Spiritualism In Focus

The fact that I can plant a seed and it becomes a flower, share a bit of knowledge and it becomes another's, smile at someone and receive a smile in return, are to me continual spiritual exercises.

LEO BUSCAGLIA

A Note about the Cover of this Book

The photo on the cover of this book was taken by Jan Budkowski of Zambezi Publishing Ltd. This beautiful spot is close to an area called Dartmeet, where the East Dart and West Dart join to form the river Dart, not that far from Ralph A. Steadman's home.

A river can symbolise many things, including the passage of time or the movement of people and goods. The bridge is even more symbolic, because it represents the link between this world and the next, or of lives already lived and those yet to come. The stones are unusual, because much of the bedrock in the UK is sedimentary. These rocks are hard, crystalline granite, the remains of a huge area of boiling magma that rose to the surface about 295 million years ago in parts of Devon and Cornwall.

The photo is interesting as well as beautful, as it connects so much with the past, the future and the ability of the earth to regenerate, and even to cope - hopefully - with changes of climate.

Spiritualism In Focus

Ralph A. Steadman

Zambezi Publishing Ltd

Published in 2020 by Zambezi Publishing Ltd,
Plymouth, Devon UK
Tel: +44 (0)1752 367 300   Fax: +44 (0)1752 350 453

British Library Cataloguing in Publication Data:
A catalogue record for this book is available
from The British Library

Cover design and illustration copyright © 2020 Jan Budkowski
Interior graphic © 2020 Gordon Johnson/Pixabay
ISBN: 978-1-903065-89-1

(Originally published in 2017 by Stellium Ltd,
as 'Spiritualism Under the Microscope')
Printed in the UK by Lightning Source

About the Author

After getting a law degree in 1954, Ralph Steadman spent nine years in the Army, mostly in Army Education. Returning to civilian life in 1963, he worked for IBM for a time, before using his computer knowledge to work in companies pioneering computerised insurance, and then computerised management of large construction projects.

In 1967, Ralph became a Training Officer in the newly formed Road Transport Industry Training Board, from which – many years later – he was 'head-hunted' to be Education and Training Manager of a large, multi-branch organisation in the retail Motor Trade. He ended his working life doing what he most loved, teaching – before retiring in 1999.

Ralph now lives in Torquay with his second wife, Sybil – a gifted clairvoyant healer – and is actively involved in local Spiritualism. He has written several books and still lectures at Spiritualist conferences. Ralph lists among his other interests, music, computers and learning languages (of which he has studied eleven, at one time or another.)

Ralph says of himself, 'For the last fifty years I have been interested in psychic phenomena in general and spiritual philosophy in particular. Over the last few years, this has expanded into the study of Metaphysics – what lies beyond Science and also Religion – which I believe is the area that contains the answers to all possible questions about the ultimate reality of life.'

Dedication.

I dedicate this book to my children – in birth order Michael, Robert, David, Ellie, Nicola and Penny. All of them, in their own different ways, have made me immensely proud to be their father.

Acknowledgments.

There are three people without whom this book would not have been produced. First I have to thank my publisher, Sasha Fenton, who originally suggested a commission for a book on mediums and mediumship. I soon realised that it was a subject which could not be considered in isolation, and so it expanded into writing about the wider environment of Spiritualism.

Next I thank Katherine Williams, an Eden Energy Medicine practitioner in Dorset. Katherine is a lovely spiritual – but non-Spiritualist – lady who attended some of my lectures at a spiritual conference in Weston-super-Mare. She kindly agreed to submit a long list of questions about Spiritualism and those questions and the answers to them have provided the backbone of this book.

Last – but by no means least – I thank Brenda Sawyer, an old friend and one of the few 'old-school' mediums left from the mid-20th Century. Brenda is an absolute goldmine of information about Spiritualism, and knew personally many of the 'big names' of the period, and her encyclopaedic knowledge, wisdom and experience – all shared with unending patience – have filled in many of the gaps in my own understanding.

Contents

Contents

3

Introduction to Spiritualism

There is an increasing interest in Spiritualism and the paranormal at the moment, and from time to time newspaper articles report strange paranormal happenings. There are even entertainment programmes on television showing mediums demonstrating their powers, or exploring ghostly happenings in some haunted house or other. However, while the more lurid events may arouse some interest, there is little knowledge about what Spiritualism really consists of, and for most people it remains a spooky off-beat religious sect with little connection to daily life.

This is not helped by the attitude of Christian churches, which uniformly condemn it. Some of the practices of Spiritualism, such as healing, are accepted as normal if practiced in a Christian church, and healing is very common in Pentecostal churches, but it is totally condemned as 'the work of the Devil' when carried out in a Spiritualist organisation. For those who think this, I would comment that exactly the same charge was made by the doctors of law against the Master Jesus, so Spiritualists are in very good company. If any answer is needed to this ridiculous idea, Christians have only to read what the Master himself said in Mark 3: 24-26. Likewise, channelling is accepted as 'prophetic utterance' in a church but condemned in any other setting.

Until now the only way of proving the truth of what Spiritualism really is has been by attending a church or a demonstration of mediumship, but this book will fill in the gap by making a simple statement about the beliefs of Spiritualists and showing what happens in a Spiritualist church or centre.

My book shows that there is nothing strange or 'spooky' about what goes on. Nothing is done in the dark or in half-light, and there is nothing frightening about the experience. In fact, it explains that Spiritualists are just the same as any other people but with slightly different beliefs.

The book is based around a series of more than fifty questions which are sometimes asked about Spiritualism. The list is not exhaustive – there are certainly many more which could be asked. For instance, there are almost twenty types of mediumship itemised under the one question 'What are the different types of mediumship?' The questions, and their answers, are 'self-standing'. That means that they can be read individually, without the need to read everything else as well. So if readers wish to look up the answer to one specific question, they can just look the question up in the Table of Contents and go to the page right away. However, this means that some information – particularly that about vibrations – slightly overlaps, as it is mentioned in the answers to several different questions.

Hopefully, the book will answer most of the questions that the reader may have about Spiritualism, and to this end it is divided up into chapters, and the questions that anyone might ask are grouped by subject. The general approach is to give simple facts, free of dogma; however, in order to explain how mediumship works, it has been necessary to give a little bit of Spiritualist philosophy, but I have kept this to a minimum and tried to put it into the simplest words possible.

For part of my professional life I was a teacher, and as a teacher I know that it is always good to use examples or 'analogies'. An analogy is something that is similar to an everyday item that everyone is familiar with. So from time to time, to clarify a particular statement, I will add an analogy to make it simple to understand. The main text deals with the subject in a 'reader-friendly' way, but for those who want to study some of the things mentioned in more depth, there is an Appendix.

For instance, Christians may be surprised to know how current Spiritualist practices mirror many events in the Bible, so the Appendix contains a list of Biblical references. The list is not exhaustive, as there are about forty separate references to the use of spiritual gifts in the New Testament alone, without mentioning the many contained in the Old Testament, but at least it will give a framework of reference for comparison.

For readers with a more scientific interest, there is also a brief résumé of scientific facts concerning vibrations, and an explanation of the Spiritualist interpretation of those facts, and for any readers who are interested in the details of Spiritualist organisations in the UK the Appendix contains details about the main ones.

There is also a short introduction to Meditation. A detailed example of its use is given in the section on how mediums are trained, but it was more appropriate to mention the basic facts about it separately.

The Appendix ends with some information about Metaphysics, which is a word that few people will have met, and even fewer understand. I leave it to the end because it puts forward the idea that the future of both Science and Religion lies in an amalgamation of both, and therefore only those who have an interest in both Science and Religion are likely to read the passage. So if you don't have that interest, just miss it out.

Finally, as I personally was brought up in a strong Christian environment – my mother was a devout member of the Church of England, and I attended church three times every Sunday from childhood until I went to University – I look at Spiritualism from that background, but I hope that my use of Christian terminology will not put off too many non-Christians.

I hope that you, the readers, may find the book instructive, and if so, that some of you may even dare to enter your local Spiritualist church or centre, and find out for yourself.
Ralph A. Steadman, June 2017

Basic Ideas

Is Spiritualism a religion or a way of life?

A religion – any religion – is a belief system, which has at its core the idea that there is some central being that was responsible for the creation of the whole Universe. A way of life is a personal code of conduct which individual human beings either choose or have forced on them. Most religions consist of both elements, and also teach of the possibility of human beings having some form of existence after the death of the physical body.

It is possible to have either element separately – humanists have their own personal code of conduct, without having the need to have a religious belief system, whereas many 'primitive' indigenous populations have a belief system without having a conscious code of conduct: they just live in harmony with Nature.

In the early days of Christianity, after the Ascension, the disciples were told to 'go and preach the Gospel' – but they were split as to what they had to preach. Some – like Thomas and James the brother of Jesus – thought that the most important thing was the moral code, the way of life that the Master had taught, whereas others – led by Peter – believed that the divinity of Jesus was the most important. Eventually, of course, the apostle Paul, who never met Jesus in the flesh, came down on the side of Peter, and the divinity of Jesus is what he taught on his travels, and what is believed by the worldwide Christian Church to this day.

The answer to this question, therefore, is that all Spiritualists believe in a central being in some form, so Spiritualism is definitely a religion, but the detailed philosophy teaches a code of conduct and morality, and explains exactly why this is important, so Spiritualism is also a way of life.

Why are so many Christians antagonistic to / fearful of Spiritualism?

Most antagonism comes from the ignorance of what Spiritualism is and a misunderstanding of what Spiritualists really do. There are all sorts of lurid stories about communing with the Devil, getting involved in Black Magic or calling up the ghosts of the dead for some sort of evil rituals – none of which are remotely true.

Much of the misunderstanding comes from the word 'spirit' itself. Whenever the word is used in the Old Testament, it is usually used to warn the Jews about avoiding evil, therefore it has nothing to do with God at all, but in one verse, (1 Samuel 16,14 – New English Bible,) the words 'an evil spirit from the Lord' appear. So God can use evil spirits. No wonder Christians are confused.

To a Spiritualist, 'spirit' is the force of creation itself, what Christians would call 'God'. Therefore, when human beings have come to the end of their physical life on Earth, the personalities return to 'spirit', the primary energy from which they came. So they are 'in spirit', and when they come back to us they are often called 'spirit friends'.

On one occasion I invited one of my sons – a Born Again Christian – to a Spiritualist service, and he actually got a message. Afterwards he had to admit that he had not seen anything evil about what had happened, and that what he had been told – that he would be doing a lot of studying – was true, although he would not be studying Spiritualism, as the medium had wrongly inferred. In fact, his only real criticism of what had happened in the service was that too much emphasis had been placed on God, and too little mention was made of Jesus.

The only way that Christians could really find out the truth about what happens would be to actually attend a Spiritualist service and see for themselves, which would remove a lot of the misunderstandings. Alternatively, of course, if that would be a little too daunting, they could invite a Spiritualist speaker or demonstrator to visit their church and speak to them.

What kinds of people are drawn towards Spiritualism?

This is as difficult a question to answer as one asking about the kind of people drawn towards any other religion. In many cases people are drawn by curiosity, or have seen a newspaper article or TV program about supernatural phenomena. Sometimes someone is at particularly low ebb in their life, and needs help and guidance on personal matters, so is persuaded to accompany a friend to a demonstration. However, probably the greatest recruiter of Spiritualism is death.

There is nothing quite like death for making someone ask what life is all about. Is death the end of everything, a complete blotting out of all that has ever happened to the dear departed? Is there anything after the funeral, or is that it? Will we ever see our loved ones again, and if so when, where and how? Why was the loved one taken at that particular time of their life? (However old or young they may have been, it was always too soon.) Is there any sort of existence after the death of the physical body, and if there is, how can we contact the loved one to find out if they are still all right?

Unfortunately, there are few ways of getting answers in such questions. If the bereaved are members of a Christian church, it may be of value to them to know that their loved one is now with Jesus in Heaven, or some such comforting thought; however, it is of no comfort at all to be told that Jesus, in his mercy, will save those who die believing in him, if the dear departed was not a Christian, or even worse, was an active atheist, in which case, of course – according to orthodox Christian theology – he/she has already gone to Hell.

Even without such extremist views, there are very few churches which can give definitive answers to most of the questions which the bereaved raise, and certainly if the answer to any question which is raised is 'That is something which no human being can understand,' it is no answer at all. However, being able to answer such questions is exactly where Spiritualism scores.

In the first place, the questioner can be shown that the loved one still exists, and just by attending one single demonstration of clairvoyance, and by talking to someone who has had a message, can realise that it is possible to still hear from them. In one amazing case which I personally witnessed, a bereaved Catholic lady friend of ours had been persuaded – a bit against her natural inclinations – to attend a demonstration, at which she received a very evidential message from her late husband. So she continued to go to the weekly demonstrations, and received similar messages, each time from a different medium, for the next seven weeks, by which time she was totally convinced of the validity of Spiritualism.

It is not only those who are new to Spiritualism who can be helped. My wife has been a Spiritualist for more than thirty years, but still grieved just as badly when her beloved mother passed away three years ago. However, less than 48 hours after she had passed, 'Mother' appeared to a young developing medium – who didn't know her – in the teaching circle of a medium friend in Canada, and said, 'Tell Carolyn – our friend – that she has to call Sybil – my wife – and tell her that I have arrived, and that I am all right.'

However, some very important recruiters to Spiritualism are the people who come along to a demonstration for the first time, and are so impressed that they tell their friends, who come also, and do the same, and so on. We have one such case at the centre to which my wife and I go weekly:

one lady came by herself last year. She still comes, but now, she is surrounded by eight of her friends and relatives each week, all of whom were first attracted by her enthusiasm.

So the answer to the question about who is attracted to Spiritualism is, 'All kinds of people, from all walks of life, and in all sorts of personal circumstances.'

Some say that it is only weak-minded people who are drawn to Spiritualism. Is that true?

This is such a silly question that it hardly merits receiving an answer at all, but in case it is thought that I can't answer it, I will.

First, let me say that there is an old saying, that 'Sarcasm is the lowest form of wit and the highest form of ignorance.' There is another one which says that 'Personal abuse is the last refuge of those who have run out of logical arguments.' So I will rise above petty insolence and mention one or two of the famous men in history who have been convinced of the validity of Spiritualism.

Sir William Crookes, (1832 – 1919).

A famous physicist and chemist, in later years he became President of the Royal Society. He was introduced to Spiritualism in his thirties, and eventually became President of the Society for Psychic Research.

Sir Oliver Lodge, (1851 – 1940).

Another famous physicist and writer, he was a Fellow of the Royal Society and principal of Birmingham University. He was also in his thirties when he was introduced to Spiritualism; by coincidence he also later became President of the Society for Psychical Research, and eventually wrote a book on Spiritualism.

Basic Ideas

Sir Arthur Conan Doyle, (1859 – 1930).
A doctor and writer of many books, including those about Sherlock Holmes, he became interested in Spiritualism in his fifties, and wrote many books about it. He apparently wished to be more remembered for his work for Spiritualism than for his fictional books.

Air Chief Marshal Lord Dowding, (1882 – 1970).
The Royal Air Force strategist of the successful defence of Britain in 'the Battle of Britain' at the beginning of the war, he had a long and distinguished career in the Royal Air Force. He became interested in Spiritualism on retirement, and wrote four books about it.

Finally, despite not ranking anywhere near any of those illustrious Spiritualists, even I have three professional qualifications, a degree in Law, a teaching qualification and a linguistics diploma, and although I have sometimes been called 'eccentric' for my beliefs, I have never yet been called 'weak-minded'.

It is said that Spiritualists invoke evil spirits: is this true?
This is no truer than saying that Christians invoke evil spirits. Both religions use prayers to call on God – or in the case of Christians, on the Master Jesus – and many Catholics invoke the names of saints. Spiritualists rarely invoke any spiritual beings, and those who do usually invoke only archangels – Michael, Raphael, Gabriel or Zadkiel – who can hardly be called 'evil spirits'.

When mediums are doing demonstrations, they are protected from evil influences by their own personal spiritual protector, known to Spiritualists as 'the Gatekeeper', but have no control whatsoever over which spirit loved ones of the congregation want to make contact, and so cannot 'invoke' them. Very often, during a private reading, a client desperately wants to hear from a particular loved one, but unless that loved one decides – and is able – to 'come through', the medium has no way of forcing them to be present.

That last statement possibly needs a bit of explaining. When we get 'to the other side of life' everything is different from what we have experienced here on earth, and so we need a period of time to get used to it. If, during his/ her physical life, a loved one 'on the other side of life' has never had any experience of communication between the 'dear-departed' and loved ones still on earth, he/ she may not know that it is possible, or how to do it if they want to, so very often they just 'sit on the side-lines' and watch it happen. In my own case, I had a very dear uncle who passed when I was at university, and he was a staunch Church of England man, who would never have thought of having anything to do with Spiritualism, so I waited in vain for more than fifty years before he eventually made contact for the first time.

Finally, in the first letter of John in the Bible, (1 John, 4.1,) we are told to 'Test the spirit, to see if it is from God', and if a medium, despite having put protection up, is in any doubt about the authenticity of any being who is trying to make contact, he/she will ask the simple question, 'Do you come in unconditional Love?' By spiritual law, that being is forced to answer truthfully, and if the answer is 'No.' then he/she/it is sent packing.

To explain that a little more fully, as John says later in the same chapter – v.9 – 'God is Love', so the question is the equivalent of asking 'Do you come in God?' and the being is therefore forced to tell the truth. Love is an interesting weapon which can be used in an emergency if someone feels that they are being attacked by an entity. Just repeat the words 'Unconditional Love', and surround yourself with the colour rose-pink – the colour vibration of Love – and you will ward the entity off, as it will not be able to stand the double expression of Love.

Spiritual Beliefs

What is the primary belief of Spiritualism?

Spiritualism is a religion and a way of life that concentrates on the survival of the personality after the death of the physical body, and not only teaches that 'Life after Death' is a fact, but actually proves it. It proves it by 'bringing through' the personalities of departed loved ones to members of the audience, and by giving enough personal information about those loved ones to convince the members that they still exist. Further proof that they are still around the members is often given by the loved ones themselves commenting on – and giving advice about – the situations that members are currently experiencing, or on interesting things which have happened to them recently.

For instance, to give an example of a very trivial - but totally evidential - bit of information which was given in a message, my wife was on holiday with relatives in Canada when she was given a message from her mother that I wasn't changing my socks, and that one of them had a hole in it. So she phoned me up and I had to admit – a bit shame-facedly – that it was true.

How does a Spiritualist's belief in God differ from that of a Christian?

All Christians worship Jesus, considering him as one of the Trinity – Father, Son and Holy Ghost – which make up the spiritual being whom they call 'God'. Spiritualists do not worship Jesus, they worship God. Just as there are different ideas about the ultimate Truth of existence expressed by all the many factions of Christianity, (Catholic, Anglican, Free Churches of various denominations, etc.) there are different views within Spiritualism. All accept the reality of a central God, although most believe that God is a force, a power, an energy – in fact Spirit – rather than a personality. In fact, there is an almost exact parallel between the Spiritualist belief and the idea of 'the Holy Spirit' in Christianity, apart from the fact that Christians believe that God and the Holy Spirit are two parts of the same being. Spiritualists believe that Spirit and God mean exactly the same thing, as does St Paul, who in 1 Corinthians 12.4-11 uses the words 'the same Spirit...the same Lord... and the same God.'

Once one goes beyond that central belief, there is a section of Spiritualism which follows the lead of the Master Jesus – Christian Spiritualism – while the main section accepts that there were spiritual masters in all religions, and all taught basic spiritual truths, so therefore it is not necessary to follow a strictly Christian pathway.

Finally, there are a few Spiritualists – of whom I am one – who believe that ultimate Truth will be found only once one brings together Science and Religion, to a point where they meet and mutually support each other. I develop this concept more in the section on Metaphysics in the Appendix.

Who, or what, do Spiritualists worship?

Most Spiritualists would say 'God', but this slightly begs the question. What does 'worship' mean? There are no prescribed rituals in Spiritualism, no formal ways of praying, or formal times of prayer, and there is no Holy Book which has to be studied, used, learnt and recited, although most Spiritualists use the Bible. There is certainly no prescribed building, or orientation of a building, which is important when carrying out an act of worship. All Spiritualists have a very strong personal code of morality and ethics, and in that they believe that they are doing the 'will of God', but the overall view of the relationship between 'God' and Mankind is totally different for Spiritualists than it is for Christians.

To most Spiritualists, God is the power, the force, the energy of Creation itself. Although usually addressed in prayer as 'Father God' – or by some, in these 'politically correct' days, as 'Father/ Mother God' – there are different views concerning the nature of God. Some consider God to be a personality, and therefore 'He', others – of whom I am one – consider that energy is non-personal, therefore should be spoken of as 'It'.

He/ It is everything which exists, every part of every life form, everything which is seen and unseen, everything manifest and un-manifest. Therefore since Mankind – we, all of us – are part of the 'everything', each of us is part of God. A minute part, obviously, an infinitesimal part compared to the massiveness of the Universe, but a part nevertheless. So the greatest form of worship that we can perform is to show – in our personal life – what God is capable of creating through human beings. Since the Master Jesus said (Matt. 22.37-40) that the first and greatest commandment is 'Thou shalt love the Lord thy God', that is what we try to do. He also stated that, 'The second is like it, namely this: Thou shalt love thy neighbour as thyself.' Therefore, as a living act of worship of God, Spiritualists try to show love to all, in whatever way they can.

It is sometimes very difficult, when as Spiritualists we are reviled by Christians and others, to remember the words of the Master, but we are fortified by the words he said, (Luke 6, 28): 'Bless them that curse you, and pray for those who despitefully use you'.

So that is what – and how – Spiritualists worship.

Do Spiritualists believe in Hell?
Yes indeed, but not the Hell of Classical literature, as portrayed in Dante's Inferno.

The Hell which exists is the Hell of being separated from the love of God. In order to explain this I need to say something about what happens after the moment of death. In order to justify this information, I have to say that it has come from the best possible source – those who have had the experience of going through the death of the physical body and who have come back to tell us about it.

There are very many scenarios to explain the possible pathways after death, but let us start with the simplest one: someone who comes to the end of a long life and passes relatively peacefully.

In this case, the personality of the individual separates from the physical body and goes directly into the Light. Why do we call it the Light? Because that is what it is, literally. Everyone who comes back to us and speaks of what we call 'the other side of life' says how bright and beautiful it is, how there always seems to be sunshine, although no sun can ever be seen. We are also told that each colour seems to be brighter than it ever was on Earth, and that some colours are seen which do not even exist in our world.

It is very interesting that when people have had NDEs – Near Death Experiences – in which they have been clinically dead for a while before being resuscitated, they talk of going along a long tube-like tunnel towards 'the Light', and then being stopped before they get there, and told to go back, as it is not their time. This has now come into everyday language, and we often say that 'there is light at the end of the tunnel.'

As an aside here, if you ever have the harrowing experience of sitting by the bedside of a loved one when he or she is about to pass over, you could tell them to 'Look for the Light'. In many cases, if they are still partially conscious and they do so, they will actually see that 'Light at the end of the tunnel' and will see their loved ones waiting in it to welcome them back 'Home'. That will then give them the kindest and gentlest passing possible, free from fear.

So that is the most common, and most important, scenario for when people pass over, but there are two other major scenarios which often happen.

One is when someone passes who is completely convinced that there is nothing at all after the death of the physical body. Now the 'other side of life' – or what is normally called 'Heaven' by Christians – is a mental realm of existence, where whatever you think is manifested immediately. So if people who pass believe that they are going into 'nothingness', then that is exactly what will happen. They enter an existence in which everything is like a grey fog around them, where nothing has any form or shape, and there they stay, until they are 'rescued' by angelic beings, who are dedicated to doing such spiritual service. They are not in Hell, just in what is sometimes called in the Catholic Church 'Purgatory', although the more normal term is 'Limbo'.

An interesting thing which was recently reported in a national newspaper was the story of a man who was an atheist, and believed that the death of the physical body was the end of existence. He had a Near Death Experience, and when he was resuscitated confidently stated that there is nothing after death, as all that he had seen was complete blackness, before coming back to consciousness. What had happened was that he had gone into the 'nothingness' which he was convinced existed. He had always imagined it as 'blackness' and that was what he had experienced. (It is an interesting question – which apparently the interviewer didn't ask – how he knew that he was in blackness, if he had no consciousness.)

However, the real 'Hell' is reserved for those who have led such evil lives that they have built up a wall of hatred for everything, for Nature, for animals, for their fellow human beings, and for God, and that wall has surrounded them and cut all possibilities of Love out of their being – and Love is the very force of creation itself. (There is a cross-reference here to

God. As the Bible says, 'God is Love', and as God is said to be the force of creation, Love is also the force of creation.)

So when such human beings pass over, they are not able to enter 'Heaven', as that is a spiritual realm of Love, and without that Love they cannot enter. So they have been condemned – or more correctly they have condemned themselves – to the living Hell of being separated from God, and there they will stay, until they also are 'rescued' by the angelic beings, who work ceaselessly, bathing them in Love, in order to gradually chip away the wall of hatred they have created round themselves. (It is a comforting fact that no-one – not even the most evil of human beings – is ever excluded permanently from 'Heaven', despite what the extremists of many religions say.)

Of course, it's not only after the death of the physical body that Hell exists – it can exist during earthly life also. When human beings say, 'I went through Hell', that is literally true, as they were going through a phase of their existence in which they felt totally cut off from all forms of Love, and so cut off from any possible connection with God. Even the Master Jesus, when on the cross, said, 'My God, my God, why hast thou forsaken me?'

There is much more which will be said later about the different scenarios which can occur after death, but here I have just answered the original question, – 'Do Spiritualists believe in Hell?' – with a resounding 'Yes'.

Is Spiritualism affected by Eastern religions?

Although there is no direct connection between Spiritualism and Eastern religions, some Spiritualists believe some aspects of Hindu and Buddhist philosophy, specifically about the energy centres of the body – the chakras – and the concept of multiple lives – Reincarnation. The latter is firmly denied by the Spiritualist National Union (SNU), although one of their principles is that of 'Compensation and Retribution hereafter for the good and evil deeds that are done on Earth'. In SNU dogma the 'hereafter' in the principle refers to a spiritual existence after the physical body has died; and although the concept of the eternal law of Cause and Effect is accepted, it is believed that the 'soul' will have time enough to reflect on what it might have done better.

Other factions of Spiritualism consider that such an idea can only lead to a belief in some sort of Hell during which souls atone for their earthly sins. Therefore a more logical idea would be to accept the Buddhist concept of 'The Wheel of Rebirth' – a series of earthly lives during which every aspect of existence as a human being is explored – until perfection is eventually reached.

As far as chakras are concerned, in the chapter on Science in the Appendix, I speak about Kirlian photography. If – as I show – it can prove the existence of meridians and acupuncture points, then there is a possibility that the existence of chakras also follows, so that the Eastern philosophy concerning them becomes a statement of physical fact. I put a section on the chakras in the Appendix, for those interested in the subject.

Does Spiritualism have anything comparable to the Ten Commandments of Christianity?
There is nothing in Spiritualism which says that followers have to believe in any doctrine or dogma, so there are no rules regarding food, dress or methods of worship. Spiritualists do have a strong personal code of morality, in common with devotees of other faiths, but the morality is best described as 'Do unto others as you would wish them to do to you', or – more commonly – 'What goes round comes round'. That is, of course, basic folk wisdom, the innate knowledge of what is right and what is wrong.

However, in 1890, one of the founder members of the modern Spiritualist movement, Emma Hardinge Britten, who was a leading medium at the time, was instrumental in drawing the various Spiritualist sects together under one national body, and in July of that year the first national conference of UK Spiritualists was held. At that conference, she proposed the adoption of a set of principles towards which all Spiritualists could aspire, and these 'Seven Principles of Spiritualism' are now accepted by all Spiritualist National Union members. They are as follows:

- The Fatherhood of God.
- The Brotherhood of Man.
- The communion of spirits and the ministry of angels.
- The continuous existence of the human soul.
- Personal responsibility.
- Compensation and retribution hereafter for all the good and evil deeds done on earth.
- Eternal progress that is open to every human soul.

Whatever the religion of any devout human being, it is difficult to find much that is objectionable in those principles, and some of them might even be accepted by those who have no religious belief at all, but have a strong moral code.

There is a different set of nine principles which are accepted in the American tradition of Spiritualism. They are as follows:

- We believe in Infinite Intelligence.
- We believe that the phenomena of Nature, both physical and spiritual, are the expression of Infinite Intelligence.
- We affirm that a correct understanding of such expression and living in accordance therewith constitute true religion.
- We affirm that the existence and personal identity of the individual continue after the change called death.

- We affirm that communication with the so-called dead is a fact, scientifically proven by the phenomena of Spiritualism.
- We believe that the highest morality is contained in the Golden Rule: "Do unto others as you would have them do unto you."
- We affirm the moral responsibility of individuals and that we make our own happiness or unhappiness as we obey or disobey Nature's physical and spiritual laws.
- We affirm that the doorway to reformation is never closed against any soul here or hereafter.
- We affirm that the precepts of Prophecy and Healing are Divine attributes proven through Mediumship.

Spiritualist Jargon

Every society in human life has its own 'jargon', words and phrases which are used in a specific sense, but which mean little or nothing to others outside that society, and Spiritualism is no different. Here are some of the phrases which are used by members, and a short interpretation of the meaning of each of them.

What does 'on the platform' mean?

This is a term used by all Spiritualists which simply means officiating at a Spiritualist service, or giving a demonstration of clairvoyance. There is a platform at the front of all churches and most centres, and so visiting mediums are physically 'on the platform' while they are performing.

What does 'sitting in circle' mean?

The strongest sort of structure in Nature is a circle, and so when Spiritualists wish to concentrate spiritual energy they normally sit round in a circle. Later in the book I will explain the way that Spiritualists conduct teaching courses, and 'sit in circle', but they also 'sit in circle' at other times. For instance, many churches have 'open circles', when any member of the public can attend, and in such circles any person present may be invited to try to give a message to someone else. It is a way of introducing people to the idea of mediumship outside the formal atmosphere of a church service or demonstration.

Another instance of 'sitting in circle' is where small groups of Spiritualists come together, often on a regular basis in a private home, in order to meditate, give and receive messages and/ or have discussions on various spiritual matters. Such circles are usually called 'closed circles', as only the regular members are invited to attend.

What is a séance?

This is a French word, which means 'meeting, session or sitting.' It was used a lot in the history of Spiritualism, when entry to demonstrations was strictly by invitation, and the whole subject was shrouded in mystery. At that time it was thought that spiritual manifestations could only take place in darkness, or at least in very dim light, and since darkness is associated in the human mind with evil, the myths of dealing with evil spirits soon began to circulate.

Spiritualists are far more enlightened today, and normally sessions are held in full light. There are, however, some advanced demonstrations where it is necessary to have subdued light, and these will be mentioned elsewhere. There are very few mediums who have the ability to give such demonstrations, so in these sessions, which are sometimes still called séances in some places, attendance is strictly limited. Therefore invitations to attend are rarely extended outside the circle of those who are already very advanced in their personal knowledge of what Spiritualism is all about. For instance, I have been actively involved in Spiritualism for more than fifty years, and there are certain types of demonstration which I have never yet had the chance to attend, although I have spoken to some people who have been fortunate enough to have experienced them, and who can vouch for their authenticity.

What is reincarnation?

Reincarnation is the belief that every human being has many different lives, during which he/she attains spiritual knowledge and experience over a long period of time. It is built into many Eastern religions, and is the cornerstone of Hinduism – arguably the oldest existing religion in the world – and of Buddhism. Reincarnation is generally dismissed by most devotees of Western religions, although there is a strong Biblical tradition of it in Judaism, and even a mention of it in the New Testament, where the Master Jesus apparently identified John the Baptist as a reincarnation of the prophet Elijah, (Matt. 17.10-13.)

Many books have been written about Reincarnation, and over recent years there have been several television programmes which have studied the subject. Probably the most evidential book ever was written by Dr. Ian Stevenson, a professor of Psychiatry, who made a life study of it. Entitled 'Twenty cases suggestive of Reincarnation', the original book is currently still available, although now very rare. However, modern re-prints are available on Amazon. He wrote two other books, the last one a very scholarly work about his research into birthmarks 'inherited' from a past life. He eventually passed away in 2007, at the grand old age of 89. For anyone interested in learning more about the subject it is worthwhile putting his name into Google, and getting references to his life and work.

What is regression?

The word regression literally means 'going back', and is used in several contexts. As far as Spiritualism is concerned, it means 'going back to a previous life, and remembering events which happened in that life.'

The most common way of regression is through hypnosis, and there are some hypnotists who specialise in it. In general, psychiatrists are sceptical about the whole idea of Reincarnation, although they accept that hypnosis can be a valid tool in psychiatry. However, there have been many studies done on supposed past lives, and some of these are very impressive.

In one Australian television programme I saw many years ago, four people, born and bred in Australia, were regressed and then were taken to the European country in which they

Spiritualist Jargon

remembered having had a past life. One of these was a man who claimed to have been a surgeon in a famous Aberdeen hospital. The records of the hospital were looked up, and a surgeon of the name claimed was indeed found, at the time in the 19th Century when the man said that he had lived. He was taken to the hospital, and immediately took the presenters on a tour round it, describing the short-cuts which he used to take from his office on his way to the operating theatres.

Then he suddenly came to a halt, totally confused, because a passage which he said he used to go down simply did not exist. So the program makers delved into the history of the hospital, and found that towards the end of the 19th century there had been a major reconstruction there, and the passage down which the surgeon used to go had been closed off. Evidence enough that his story was correct.

What does 'psychic' mean?
The word 'psychic' comes from the Greek word for 'soul', so that quite simply it means 'anything to do with the soul'. In the mind of most Spiritualists it is the same as the word 'spiritual', but there is a distinction made when speaking of mediums, and the way in which they work.

If you concentrate on anyone whom you do not know, you will very often find that you can start to get impressions about them, about what sort of character they have, what they are thinking, whether or not they are antagonistic to you, and similar ideas. Non-Spiritualists usually call this 'using your intuition', or 'reading someone's character'. Most mediums are very good at picking up these impressions, and when they do so we say that they are 'working on the psychic'. This is different to 'working spiritually', as the latter means contacting the spirit friends or loved ones of a person here on Earth, and relaying messages which they wish to give.

We say elsewhere that a medium is like a telephone exchange operator, who receives messages, sorts them out and directs them to the appropriate recipient. However, what happens when no messages are coming through?

In this case most mediums will choose one person in the audience and will start to 'work on the psychic' with him/ her, picking up some of their existing thoughts or conditions, or the current family environment around them. Doing this will almost always prompt the loved ones of that person, 'on the other side of life' to draw close and to want to give messages, at which time the medium just switches over to working spiritually as normal.

It may also be argued that the word 'spiritual' should be used only when spiritual beings, or departed loved ones, are involved, so therefore anything which is not directly connected with those 'on the other side of life' should be classed as 'psychic' and not 'spiritual'. However, as far as most non-spiritualists are concerned, 'psychic' and 'spiritual' can be considered as meaning exactly the same thing, so if you are new to Spiritualism, just accept that as a fact, and let others argue over technicalities if they wish.

What is an aura? Can it be seen?
An aura is a force-field of electrical energy which surrounds the whole body. It cannot normally be seen, unless the person is psychic, but it certainly can be felt by most people, whether psychic or not. The electrical energy of the body is highly concentrated around the head, and in Biblical times many ordinary people could see this around the heads of the apostles: this why in all Christian paintings the apostles and the Master Jesus himself were always portrayed as having a halo of light round their heads. I enlarge on this theme later in the Appendix, when talking about the chakras.

Spiritualist Practices

How are evil forces kept out of Spiritualist services?

Well, I will answer this question with another: how are they kept out of Christian services? I would imagine that the answer would be, by prayer and by invocation – and the same applies to Spiritualist services.

Christians are familiar with the word 'prayer', of course, as they use formula prayers in every service – they are part of the appropriate prayer-book – but they might be a little more dubious about the word 'invocation', so I will explain it.

The word comes from two Latin words, 'in' and 'vocare', which together mean 'calling-in', and we can call in any spiritual being as and when we wish. Anyone in the Catholic Church is well aware of this, of course, as they frequently 'call in' various saints for specific purposes. For instance, the Virgin Mary might be invoked by a woman for protection during childbirth, or St. Christopher by a traveller making a difficult journey. St. Martin of Tours is often invoked to help people with financial problems, and there are a whole host of saints who may be invoked and asked to perform miracles in the lives of those in need of help. In fact, invocation is built into the very fabric of Catholic theology, as a number of documented cases of miracles done by a departed human being are needed to qualify that person for consideration for being made a saint.

Built into Christian rituals and prayers are invocations of the Master Jesus or of God, for protection of all kinds, and I can still remember, as a child, being terrified by one invocation during prayers in my Anglican church for 'protection against 'the world, the flesh and the Devil'.

Therefore the short answer to the question is, 'by the same methods as in Christian churches, by prayer and by invocation'. However, while talking about invocations, let me enlarge on the theme slightly.

Spiritual Law says that if spiritual beings are invoked by calling their name three times, they are forced to be present, and even the greatest of spiritual beings cannot refuse to obey the summons. I myself use invocations frequently, sometimes of angels but more often of archangels. I will give four examples of this:

Michael: the Archangel Michael is often called 'The Lord Michael', as he is the Lord of the Heavenly Host, so his main function is Protection. He can be invoked for either physical protection, when a person is facing imminent physical danger, or for spiritual protection against any possible negative entities. He can also be invoked for psychic protection when going into situations of sickness – into hospital surroundings, for instance.

Raphael: the Archangel of healing. He is routinely invoked when there is an illness or long-standing physical or mental condition for which help is sought.

Zadkiel: the Archangel of Transmutation. This Archangel is in charge of one of the rays of creation, the violet ray, and is invoked to clear all negative energies from a place, condition or round a person. I had an interesting example of his power recently:

A lady contacted me late at night to say that she had just had a phone call from a friend of hers, 200 miles away, who had had a massive emotional shock, and was ringing her to virtually say goodbye, as she was about to commit suicide. The lady pleaded with her not to do it, but she rang off –

and the lady asked if I could help. I immediately invoked Zadkiel and asked him to 'surround the friend with the violet flame of Transmutation, to transmute all negative energy into Love, the highest form of Light, and release it for the benefit of the universe'.

The next morning the friend phoned the lady again, who asked where she was. She said that she was at home, as the night before, just after she had rung off, she had felt a wave of calmness flooding into her, and all thoughts of ending her life had just vanished away, so she had driven home in an aura of total peace and love.

Finally I invoke **Gabriel**, the Archangel of Divine guidance and inspiration. He is famous in both Christian and Islamic theology as a divine messenger, as he was reputed to have brought the Virgin Mary the news that she was to be the mother of the Master Jesus, and also to have dictated the Koran to the prophet Mohammed.

I had a most amazing demonstration of his power earlier this year. I was at a Spiritualist conference, and had been booked to give four talks, of an-hour-and-a-half each. Three of them were talks I had never given before, and the fourth was a composite of two talks which I had given three years ago, of which I still had the notes.

I had no problem at all with the first two, and soon learnt them off by heart, and I needed only to take the notes for the fourth into the lecture room in order to give it, but I had problems with the third: I couldn't get it right. I worked on it for two weeks, and even typed it out, word for word – all thirty-five pages of it – but it still wasn't right. I didn't know what was wrong, but I knew that I couldn't give that lecture.

Finally, in desperation, twenty minutes before the scheduled start of the lecture, I invoked Gabriel, and asked for his assistance and inspiration. I was immediately calmed down and reassured, and then went into the lecture room. As soon as I started, I abandoned all my notes, and gave an off-the-cuff lecture, which was probably one of the best I have ever given. It covered most of the material which I had intended to cover – with the exception of one section, which I missed out completely. I was told afterwards by a medium friend that there had been a lady in the audience who would have been seriously wounded emotionally had I talked about that subject, but Gabriel had skilfully helped me to avoid it.

Do Spiritualists all take part in séances?
The modern version of séances, apart from those which I have mentioned above, is 'sitting in circle'. Whether the circles are public – 'open circles' – or private – 'closed circles' – there are relatively few Spiritualists who 'sit' regularly – in fact, usually only those who have deliberately decided that they want to develop any potential gifts that they may have. The majority are quite content to attend a church, or go to weekly demonstrations of clairvoyance at a local centre.

Do all Spiritualists get involved in regression?
Although most Spiritualists know about regression, few have ever been regressed, for one very good reason. The biggest and most important Spiritualist organisation in the United Kingdom, the Spiritualist National Union, doesn't believe in Reincarnation, so the whole subject is never mentioned in SNU churches, and it is unlikely that SNU members would ever want to be regressed. For the remainder, the thought of recalling past lives might be of passing interest, but it is of far less interest than establishing, here and now, the fact of the survival of the personality of departed loved ones.

However, despite not being consciously involved in regression, many people – and not only Spiritualists – occasionally experience 'spontaneous regression'. This happens when someone suddenly has a memory of being in a different life, in a different time and/or in a different country.

All of us, from time to time, meet people to whom we feel drawn from the moment of our first meeting. We may even say 'We get on like a house on fire.' There are others, of course, whom we hate from the start, without having any rational explanation of why we do so. When this happens, there is a very good possibility that we have a 'Karmic link' with those people – we are sub-consciously remembering relationships from a past life. If the feeling is particularly strong, sometimes by meditating on the person we can get impressions about a previous life in which we were together, and these impressions are commonly called 'flashbacks'.

I myself have had many such experiences, and there are three people in my life at present – including my wife and our closest friend – with whom I can remember having had different relationships in past lives.

How does a Spiritualist church differ from other churches?

The main physical difference in a church is that there is no altar. At the front of the church there is a raised platform, usually railed in and with flowers round it, on which the 'chairman/ woman' sits with the medium who is going to demonstrate. There are rarely pews: rows of individual chairs are the usual arrangement. If it is a Christian Spiritualist church, there will be a cross prominent somewhere at the front, while in a Spiritualist National Union church there will be a wall plaque or tablet on the front wall showing the 'Seven Principles of Spiritualism'.

However, there are a large number of Spiritualist centres, which are not formal churches. Spiritualists believe that it is not necessary to have a formally dedicated church in order to be able to worship. (In fact, there is very good scriptural backing for this view: in Matthew 18.20 the Master Jesus said that where two or three gather in his name, he is in the midst of them.) Spiritualists believe that God is everywhere, so can be worshipped anywhere.

As an aside here, that belief is held by not only Spiritualists, nor even by just Christians: it is also held by other religions. There is a lovely story told about a famous Sikh guru, a teacher who travelled round India teaching, and slept out of doors most nights. One morning he was woken up by angry villagers, who accused him of insulting their God as he had slept with his feet facing their temple. (Pointing the feet at anyone was held to be a sign of disrespect.) His wise reply was, 'Show me where God is not, and I will point my feet in that direction.

Therefore for a Spiritualist any hall or room anywhere, ideally – but not necessarily – with a raised platform, can be used in order to hold a service or demonstration. There are many Spiritualist centres in the Torbay area, most of which are in community centres of one kind or another, but the one which my wife and I ran for many years was, and still is, held in the function room of a pub.

Although many religious people will be totally scandalised at that idea, we have found that it has had one very great advantage. Many non-religious people who would never dream of setting foot in a church – housewives, workmen, students, tourists or just casual visitors – are often intrigued by the idea of being able to have a drink while watching a demonstration, and – in the famous words of Oliver Goldsmith – 'some who came to scoff remained to pray'.

People are able to sit and watch the demonstration in a relaxed atmosphere, far removed from the formal surroundings of a church, and so are more able to understand that their loved ones 'on the other side of life' enjoy an existence which, in all cases, is far better than the one which they had on Earth ever was. What is more, they are enjoying it now, and are not asleep and having to wait until some time in the distant future, when 'the trumpet shall sound and the dead shall be raised' for it to happen.

The other great advantage, of course, lies in the fact that if the 'dear-departed' relative wasn't an active church-goer, it would be stretching the imagination a bit for the loved ones still on earth to think of him/ her 'coming through' in a church, whereas even church-goers will occasionally go to a pub at some time or other during their life, if only for family celebrations.

Does one have to be invited to join a Spiritualist church?

Anyone can attend a service in a Spiritualist church or centre. You just walk in at the door and sit down. If you eventually become interested in what happens, and wish to find out more about it, then you can apply to join and become a member of the church, pay a subscription and that is it. The benefits of joining are that you would be able to use the library and may apply to sit in whichever closed circles – teaching circles – are being currently held. Of course, once a member and attending regularly then you are more likely to meet and get to know some long-term Spiritualists who will be able to answer any questions you may ask.

In common with all Christian churches, a 'collection' – or 'free-will offering' – is taken during the service to help with the expenses of running the church. However, if one goes to a public demonstration of clairvoyance, there is usually a fixed entrance fee, and this is the normal practice in most Spiritualist centres.

What is the normal format of a Spiritualist church service?

The majority of the service is very little different to what happens in a Christian church. It usually starts with the chairman/ woman introducing the speaker for the night; it is customary for Spiritualist mediums to travel round from church to church rather than demonstrate at the same church or centre every week. The medium then leads the congregation in prayer, including prayers for the protection of everyone present, and a hymn is sung. Next, the medium gives a spiritual reading which he/ she has chosen specially for the night. The reading may be from the Bible, or any other spiritual source, such as a poem or piece of inspirational writing, and this is followed by another hymn.

The medium then gives a spiritual address, similar to a church sermon, which may be on any subject, possibly referring to the challenges of modern living, possibly a commentary on a Biblical saying or proverb, but usually tied in with the previously chosen reading. This is followed by another hymn.

Now comes the major difference between Christian and Spiritualist services – the clairvoyance. This is a period during which the medium will see/ hear/ sense (or a mixture of all three,) the spirit forms – the personalities – of departed loved ones who wish to 'come through' and give messages of hope and comfort to those who are in the congregation.

Messages usually last for about five minutes each: the first part is for the medium to describe the spirit form of the loved one – the communicator – physically and by character. Sometimes mediums know which member of the audience the message will be for, sometimes they don't. In the latter case, they will ask if any member of the congregation can understand the description of the person who is showing him/ herself. If they can't, the medium will give more information until the loved one is recognised or 'accepted'.

The message which the loved one wishes to give is then passed on: it may be advice about a current situation in the member's life, or about how to deal with a family member. It may be something as mundane as 'Fix that loose step before it causes an accident.' or 'It's about time you stopped smoking so much.' On the other hand, it may be a memoir of some amusing event in the life of the departed loved one – something which no-one else but the member would understand.

It may be something about meeting another departed family member or friend – for instance, 'I have met up with Aunty Jean' - and the message usually ends with the communicator expressing their love, and possibly leaving a little spiritual present – a favourite flower or even a box of chocolates.

Sometimes the message which is given is not for the person present at all, but for some member of their family who is in need, and in that case the member is asked to pass on the message to the appropriate person. There are some particularly poignant examples of this when the communicator is a child, who leaves the message, 'Tell Mummy and Daddy that I am alright now, and not in pain any longer.' Very often, in such cases, there isn't a dry eye anywhere in the room by the end of the message.

In my life as a Spiritualist, I have sat in on more than a thousand services or demonstrations, and heard somewhere between five and eight thousand messages, but I have never yet heard any communicator say that he or she would want to be back on Earth – because they wouldn't. The existence which they have now is so much better than anything they might have ever known when on Earth.

The medium is then 'called to time' by the chairman/chairwoman, and the service ends with a final hymn and a blessing.

One occasionally sees two mediums on the platform at the same time. As all mediums may have different gifts, some feel more at ease doing one type of spiritual work than another. For instance, in my case, I have never been either clairvoyant or clairaudient; I do have some degree of clairsentience, although not enough to demonstrate on the platform. However, my main spiritual interest has always been in the philosophy of Spiritualism – what life is all about, and how and why things happen – and as I have the gift of speaking and channelling I have often given talks and lectures on spiritual philosophy. Sometimes I have worked on the platform with a clairvoyant medium, and have given the spiritual address in a service, while the medium followed on to give the clairvoyance.

Quite often a husband and wife are both mediums, and work together on the platform, one giving the spiritual address – the philosophy – and the other doing the clairvoyance. If both are clairvoyant, sometimes they will alternate giving messages, while at others they may 'tune in' to each other, and do a kind of 'double-act', both concentrating on the same link and adding whatever they pick up individually to the same message.

Another variation is where two people have trained together and have become firm friends, so that when they start working spiritually they work together on the platform, either alternating or tuning in to each other.

Looking back on what I have just said about the normal format of a Spiritualist service, it is difficult to find anything remotely evil or harmful in it – and certainly nothing connected with the Devil or Black Magic. That is because there is nothing which happens which can bring anything but light and comfort into the life of the members of the congregation who received the messages – and also hope and understanding for the newly-bereaved.

A different spiritual evening is where the medium gives a demonstration of clairvoyance only. This is more of a social evening than a service: the medium is welcomed by the chairman/ woman, and will open in prayer, following on directly by demonstrating clairvoyance for an hour or so. This is probably followed by a healing meditation, during which prayers are said for anyone in need, and particularly for those listed in the 'Healing Book' for that night.

The medium then closes in prayer, and a variety of things will follow. There are always free refreshments available, and – if required – free healing sessions with one of the healers of the centre, private – paying – readings with one or other of the mediums present, free personal and/or bereavement counselling or just general social conversation.

In the centre to which we go – Infinity Clairvoyance, in Torquay – there are always half a dozen or more healers present each night, and at least the same number of mediums – on one night there were twelve – so there is plenty of choice available for those who wish to take advantage of their services. Many members have their 'favourite' healer or medium, and visit them regularly. There are also senior Spiritualists who are available to give free spiritual counselling and general advice for anyone in need, and particularly to those who are still grieving for the recent loss of a beloved relative. This is why 'Infinity' is now one of the leading Spiritualist centres in the area.

Guides and Inspirers

What is the difference between a guide and an inspirer?
Before I answer this, let me say that all men and women have guides and inspirers, who can be either male or female. However, to avoid saying 'he/ she' and 'her/ him' continually I will just talk about men and male guides.

Every person has two spiritual beings who attach themselves to him permanently. Spiritualists believe that the whole universe is based on Love, and the greatest way of showing Love is through service to others – and what better spiritual service could one give than guiding someone through all the problems of human life. To us, the prospect of binding oneself to the service of someone for what could be up to a hundred years or so would be intolerable, but since in the spirit world time does not even exist – a thousand years are just like the blink of an eyelid – that is no problem.

The principal spiritual being is the main guide, who in some branches of Christianity is called 'the guardian angel' – although he will not be an angel: he will be the perfected soul of someone who has gone through many human lives, and learned all the lessons which could be possibly learnt as a human being. The main guide, sometimes called 'the Doorkeeper' by Spiritualists, is there to remind us of the ideal pathway through life, the best way to conduct ourselves in our personal life and towards others.

Everyone is aware of the idea of 'a conscience', and so the main guide can be thought of as our conscience. In a previous book I likened him to the 'conscience' of Pinocchio, in the wonderful children's tale, who was personified as Jiminy Cricket and who continually tried to keep Pinocchio on the straight and narrow – but didn't always succeed. So perhaps we can think of our main guide as our own personal 'Jiminy Cricket'. He certainly has just as difficult a job keeping us on the right path as Jiminy Cricket did with Pinocchio, and he doesn't always succeed, either.

The other spiritual being who is with us permanently is normally called our 'Gatekeeper'. He is the one whose job is to protect us from any harmful spiritual influences, and he particularly guards us when we are doing any spiritual work, such as mediumship. For instance, when a medium brings through a loved one to a client, other loved ones no longer in a physical body are often so excited at the possibility of contacting the person on Earth that they all try to crowd in at once – and the Gatekeeper has to keep them under control, very much like a bouncer in a night club.

However, neither of those two spiritual beings can override our own personal wishes, and in the case of the Gatekeeper, if we have deliberately or unwittingly invited in some harmful being, he can do nothing about it but stand aside and watch. After all, if you have a personal bodyguard standing at the door of your own home, that bodyguard doesn't stop your invited guests coming in, does he?

So those are our permanent guides, but there are many others who will normally be with us for only part of our life. Each guide is in charge of a specific spiritual gift: for instance, a healing guide – usually a former doctor or surgeon – will help us when we are healing, a speaking guide – usually a former teacher of some sort – when we are giving a spiritual address, a clairvoyant/ clairaudient/ clairsentient guide during demonstrations of mediumship, and so on.

So why are these guides only with us during part of our life, and not for the whole of it? Because as we become more proficient at using whatever gifts we have, we need higher-level guides to take us on further, and teach us more. It is very easy to understand this by thinking of what happened to you at school: when you had learned all that you had to be taught in the syllabus for any one year, you went up into the next class, and had a different teacher, who taught the syllabus for that year, and took you up to the next level.

In the spiritual realms all human ideas of importance, prestige, status, etc. have been left behind, and when a guide realises that he has taught the person as much as he can, he just steps back and allows another guide to come in. I personally am inspired in my spiritual writing by a 'committee' of guides, all of whom move in and out effortlessly to add their little bit of wisdom at an appropriate time. I have no way of knowing when the changes are going to happen, although I sometimes feel a slight change of energy when another guide takes over.

However, apart from these guides, all of whom are associated with a specific gift, we have others who help us from time to time, and inspire us to act in one certain way, rather than another. Sometimes they come to us when we are at crossroads in our life, and have decisions to make, but not only then: all of us receive inspiration from time to time, and have what we call 'good ideas' – and these are the result of our inspirers working with us to bring some sort of change into our lives.

Finally, we have beings who are with us from time to time, who try to add their own spiritual energy to help us in various ways, possibly to cheer us up, or to look at situations in slightly different ways when we are confused. These are normally called 'helpers', and very often are our own loved ones who are now 'on the other side of life', but who are still trying their best to help us overcome the many problems of daily life. (In my own case, it is almost certain that 'Auntie Margaret' is still around me, looking after her 'spiritual son').

Spiritual Protection

What is 'spiritual protection', and why is it needed?

When one is learning any new skill, part of the training always consists of finding out all the physical dangers inherent in working with the tools or the materials which are involved in using that skill, and there is little difference in principle between that and learning about how to use spiritual skills.

However, the big difference between learning a skill in a trade or profession and learning a spiritual skill lies in the fact that spiritual skills operate in areas which are beyond the physical world, and therefore touch on dangers which are appropriate to those areas, and are little understood in our world.

Elsewhere I have said that psychic sensitivity is very close to the emotional level of the human being – the emotional body – which is not too far from the mental level – the mental body – and unless care is taken, trying to achieve spiritual skills can very seriously affect either body. All of us know of instances where someone has become so spiritually devout, in his or her own religion, that they have become emotionally and mentally completely deranged, and have totally lost all ability for rational thinking. In fact, the difference between 'devotion' and 'bigotry' or 'fanaticism' can be remarkably small. The most obvious cases of this, of which we are seeing all too many at the moment in our world, are where religious fanatics have been prepared to blow themselves up, ideally with as many other people as possible, to show their devotion to their god.

So that I am not accused of being biased against any one religion here, let me point out that exactly the same thing happened in the Middle Ages, where the Christian Church of the time committed genocide by exterminating the Cathars, a 'heretic' Christian sect in Southern France. On one occasion, where the crusading troops had captured a city, and were about to slaughter all the inhabitants, men, women and children, the spiritual leader was asked how they could differentiate between the true believers – who naturally ought to be spared – and the heretics, who were to be killed. He replied with the immortal words, 'Kill them all. God will know his own.'

In both of the examples cited above, striving for spiritual ideals led to the worst kind of religious bigotry, because lower-level energies came in and perverted the whole purpose of the spiritual mission. So that is why we need to find out how to protect ourselves before we try to learn any spiritual skill.

Regrettably, in all religions, there is a very thin line between devout behaviour and bigotry. The more that most people are involved in their own religion or religious sect, the less likely they are to accept that others have different views to them, despite worshipping the same God. For instance, Islam has been split for the last 1300 years between Sunnis and Shias due to arguments about who was the rightful successor of the prophet Mohammed, and fanatics on both sides are prepared to kill those on the other side without any further justification than that. Also in Christianity there has been hatred between Catholics and Protestants, leading to 'wars of religion' in the past. Another example is how many devout Christians, although professing to follow the Master Jesus, totally forget his command 'Love ye one another, as I have loved you.' when it comes to considering those of other faiths – or even thinking about Spiritualists.

So that is why anyone who is thinking of trying to learn a spiritual skill needs to learn something about protection first.

There are several ways of protecting oneself against harmful energies, of which the following are the most used:

Imagine yourself being surrounded by a huge balloon, and then fill that balloon with brilliant white light and continually be aware, whatever you are doing throughout the day, that you are surrounded by that light.

An alternative way is to once more imagine that you are in a balloon, but this time plate the outside of the balloon with mirror tiles, all facing outwards, so that any harmful energy which is directed towards you is automatically reflected away. (This is particularly effective if you feel that someone is actively directing evil towards you, in some Satanic or Black Magic ritual or other, such as voodoo.)

The final way is to invoke a spiritual being, usually Lord Michael – the Archangel Michael, who is Lord of the Heavenly Hosts, whence his title. To invoke Lord Michael, call his name three times, and by spiritual law he will be forced to be with you. Then ask him to surround you with protection: it is a common visualisation to imagine yourself surrounded by a blue cloak – sapphire blue is the colour associated with Lord Michael – and ask him to cut away all evil from round you. Once more a common visualisation is to imagine a blue sword cutting through a swathe of black threads around you, leaving you completely free in the centre. The actual wording is immaterial: what is important is the intention. However, the final invocation in full might be as follows:

'Lord Michael, Lord Michael, Lord Michael, I ask you to be with me now. I ask you to surround me with your blue cloak of protection and with your blue sword, cut away all influences from me which may be harmful. This I ask in the name of the First and Prime Creator, the one whom we all serve.'

Is spiritual protection needed if one is not a Spiritualist?

As we have said elsewhere every human being has an aura, and that aura can extend several feet beyond the physical body. So it is inevitable that, as we all live our daily lives, our own aura will overlap with those of other people. This is so normal that we very rarely feel anything, but occasionally, when we come into conditions of sickness, our aura will start to sense the condition in the aura of the person who is sick, and if we stay close to them for any length of time we will start to experience the condition ourselves. It will not show itself immediately in the physical body, but we may well start to feel it as a vague unease in our emotions. This is well-known, for instance, where people are caring for a sick relative over a long period of time: after a while, they will start to feel completely drained emotionally.

Earlier, I have mentioned invoking Zadkiel wherever there are negative energies – and there are certainly a lot of those around conditions of long-term sickness. So if you are caring for someone in that situation it might be a good idea to invoke Zadkiel each morning, with the following words:

'Zadkiel, Zadkiel, Zadkiel, I ask you to be with me now. I ask you to surround......(the patient) and this whole house with the violet flame of Transmutation, to transmute all negative energies into Love, the highest form of Light, and release it for the benefit of the Universe.'

However, whether or not you yourself are in such a situation, it is always a very good practice to use one or other of the methods of protection at the start of each day. If you have a daily morning routine of prayer, build it into your routine; if not, make a special effort to start each day with protecting yourself, and then you can feel completely safe for the rest of the day, wherever you go.

What is Mediumship?

What is a medium?

The word medium is a Latin word meaning 'middle', so a medium is an 'in-between', an interpreter, or a passer-on of messages. The best way to think of a medium is as an operator in a telephone exchange, who receives incoming messages and then has to sort them out and pass them on to the appropriate recipient. However, we need to know where these messages are coming from, and from whom.

This is where we have to go into a little bit of spiritual philosophy. Every human being is composed of two elements, a physical body and a personality. The physical body can be recognised by using one or other of the physical sensory organs, the skin, tongue, nose, ears or eyes, which are respectively the organs of touch, taste, smell, hearing and sight, but the personality cannot be recognised by any of those organs, because the personality is non-physical.

Scientists tell us that everything in creation has an energy, and this energy is measured by the level of vibrations which it gives off. For instance, copper gives off a different vibration to silver, and that of gold is different to both of them, and so on.

So each physical body gives off vibrations at a certain level; but the personality also gives off a vibration, at a far higher level than that of the physical body. The predominant vibration of the personality is that of the 'mental body', which is the frequency of pure thought, but as it is held closely within the physical body it can operate within only a very limited range while the human being is 'alive'.

To understand what happens after the moment of physical death, it is a useful analogy to think of what happens to a helium balloon. When the balloon is filled with helium, it tries to rise up, to a level where the density of the balloon is equal to that of the air outside. If released it will rise up until it reaches that level, where it will stay until it eventually bursts.

In the same way, at the moment of the death of the physical body, the personality separates from the body and rises to the vibrational level of pure thought. This is the level which Spiritualists call 'the other side of life', or what is normally called 'Heaven'. At this level the frequency of its own vibrational level is equal to the 'outside' level, and so that is where the personality stays. This frequency is so high in our dimension that it can no longer be sensed by any of the five physical senses of human beings. (It is an interesting fact that in most cultures 'Heaven' is often thought as 'up in the sky': it is certainly 'up' – up at the top of the frequencies in our dimension.)

However, all human beings have other senses apart from those physical ones. Many of us can walk into a room and feel the vibrations of the personalities of people within the room. Some of us feel uneasy when we think of a certain event which is going to take place in the future, or know intuitively which road to take when driving through an unknown landscape. All of these are examples of the use of senses which are not physical, and so are usually called 'psychic', but most non-Spiritualists normally use words like 'intuition', 'gut-feeling' or – in modern slang – 'vibes'.

Just as there are the five physical senses, associated with physical organs, the same senses are duplicated on a higher vibrational level, and are associated with psychic – non-physical – organs in the body – the chakras. The three higher senses which are most common are clairsentience, clairaudience and clairvoyance. The three words all have French origins. The French word 'clair' means 'clear', so 'clairsentience' means 'clear-feeling', 'clairaudience' mean 'clear-hearing' and 'clairvoyance' means 'clear-seeing'.

Now just as all of us have different sensitivity of the physical organs, in other words some of us can feel, hear or see better than others, some people have greater sensitivity in their psychic organs, and we call these people 'psychics'. Mediums are people who have their psychic abilities developed to a high level, at which they can use them at will.

So how do mediums use their enhanced psychic abilities? Well, as we have said, after the moment of death, the personality exists at the vibrational level of pure thought, and it is to that vibrational level that the psychic gifts of mediums are tuned. Some are tuned to the lower layer and so they can only 'sense' personalities, others are tuned to the next layer, and so they 'hear' them, while others are tuned to the top layer, and so they 'see' them. There are a few rare individuals who have gifts tuned to all three vibrational levels, and so can feel, hear and see personalities at the same time.

Therefore, in a service or demonstration, a medium will connect with the personalities of departed loved ones, and will pass on to the members of the congregation or audience whatever messages those loved ones wish to give.

What is the difference between a medium and a clairvoyant?

As we have said, a medium is a person who has enhanced psychic gifts, whereas a clairvoyant is a person who has enhanced gifts of 'clear-seeing'. So therefore, the word 'medium' is really an 'umbrella term' for a whole group of psychics, whereas 'clairvoyant' is a psychic with a specific gift. However, most people don't really understand the difference, so the two terms are often used indiscriminately, even by Spiritualists, who ought to know better.

Are there any mediums who are not clairvoyant?

Yes indeed, and for a very good reason. Apart from the psychics whom we have mentioned above, there are those with different skills altogether – or at least with skills which are particular examples of clairsentience.

The most obvious example of mediums who may not be clairvoyant are healers. These psychics are able to 'plug in' to the universal healing force, (or 'God', whatever that means in your mind-set) and able to direct healing to the parts of the patient's body or mind where it is needed. These mediums are highly sensitive, but not all are clairvoyant, although after a period of using their healing gifts many do, in fact, develop clairvoyance.

Another example is a medium who is a psychometrist. Psychometry is a special form of clairsentience, and is discussed in detail later in the book, so I won't enlarge on the theme here.

Yet another is an inspirational speaker, who receives information from his/ her spiritual helpers, and is inspired what to say to the audience. A special case of this is a channelling medium, who allows himself to be taken over by the spiritual being, and has no control whatsoever about what is said.

These are the different kinds of mediums one normally finds in Spiritualist churches or centres, but there are other kinds of mediumship practised outside religion as well. For instance, there are Tarot readers, who use the cards as focal points to allow them to meditate and pick up psychic information about the clients. However, in passing on information gained from non-terrestrial sources, they are effectively acting as mediums as well.

One interesting way of getting information through paranormal methods is through dowsing. This is also a form of clairsentience, where the dowser picks up the vibrations of whatever is being dowsed – traditionally it was water, but many other things are possible – and those vibrations are received and interpreted subconsciously in the brain, which causes minute changes in the muscles, thereby moving the rods, twigs or pendulums – or whatever the dowser is using – and passing on information.

I once went on a dowsing weekend, where we learnt various forms of dowsing, and did a number of prepared exercises, which proved to everyone's satisfaction that dowsing ability is possessed by most of the population.

So to go back to the original question, there are a great number of forms of mediumship, and clairvoyance is only one of them.

Can anyone be a medium?

All human beings have one or more spiritual gifts, although very few of them know the fact. After all, if you don't even know that spiritual gifts exist, you are not likely to try to find out what gifts you have, are you? Also, for those who are interested, it is very difficult to find out what their own particular gift might be.

If you want to find out what your own particular gift is, the best way to do so is to consult a medium, but this in itself usually presents a problem. There are a large number of mediums in the world, and regrettably not all of them are genuine – or even spiritual. Many are complete charlatans, whose only skill is that of extracting money out of gullible clients. Also the growth of internet advertising has meant that such people have an almost endless supply of potential victims.

Let me say here and now that there are very many genuine mediums who advertise on the internet and who have no connection with any church or centre, but the problem is that anyone who is seeking help has no way of knowing which are the genuine ones and which are not. Possibly the best way of finding a genuine independent medium is to ask round friends and acquaintances, and find out if any have ever visited or consulted one: after all, personal experience is the best recommendation.

Failing that, the best way for anyone who is seeking spiritual help is to go to a Spiritualist church or centre and ask for advice. All of these will have a list of reliable local mediums, and most churches offer a service through which bookings for readings can be made. In many local centres there is often a 'one-to-one' service offered, where someone can have a short time – 5 to 10 minutes – with any medium there on the night, for a small fee. This is not long enough to go into much detail, but it is certainly long enough for the medium to tell the client what spiritual gifts or talents he/she may have, and give advice how to develop them.

All people are born with some spiritual gift or other, but it is very often seen that many people, who later become Spiritualists, don't become aware of their gifts until they are in their forties, by which time they will have had some experience of life, and will be less subject to 'flights of fantasy'. However, there is a well-known spiritual saying that, 'When the pupil is ready, the master will appear', and so at the appropriate time someone will come into the life of those who are destined to develop mediumistic gifts, and will then start them on their spiritual journey.

Can both men and women become mediums?

Yes, indeed. Mediumship is not normally thought of as a male occupation, but some of the top mediums in the world are men. However, there is a lot of difference between ability and inclination.

It has always been known that boys and girls are naturally attracted to different careers: there are not a lot of girls who have a burning ambition to become plumbers, electricians, engineers or firemen, while few men are interested in becoming nurses or secretaries. I had a long career as a Training Officer in the Motor Trade and in conjunction with a local college set up a scheme to screen applicants for technical apprenticeships. In all the years that the scheme was running, and all the thousands of applications that we processed, we saw only one from a girl – and that was for the rarest of all trades – that of a motor-cycle mechanic.

The same thing applies in Spiritualism: there are relatively few men who are interested in it – it somehow doesn't seem manly to take an interest in the subject. My wife and I have run demonstrations of clairvoyance for many years, and out of a weekly audience of thirty to forty people, there are rarely more than five or six men present. Also, although we have started many people on the road to mediumship, we have never yet had a man in a development circle - and I believe that groups training mediums in other churches or centres don't often have men on their courses either.

So the short answer to the question is that both men and women can train to become mediums if they want to. In the last chapter of this book, on 'The scientific background', I look at the difference in 'right- and left-brain activity', which considers the subject in much more detail.

Can anyone learn how to be a medium by reading a book?

The short answer is 'No.' Not only is it not possible, but it is also very dangerous. Psychic sensitivity is closely allied to emotions, and if someone has emotional issues, or is in a weak mental or emotional state, trying to contact higher-level energies can be very upsetting, and the person doing so runs the risk of contacting lower-level energies and not being able to control them. So the best advice is to accept that no form of mediumship is a 'Do-it-yourself' matter, and to be suspicious of books which try to persuade you that it can be done safely.

Mediums talk about 'links': what are they?

We have said that a medium acts like an operator in a telephone exchange. Sometimes telephone callers say exactly who the person is to whom they want to speak, in which case the operator's job is easy, but sometimes they have a general question which cannot immediately be routed to a specific department, and so the operator has to ask around to find out who is the best person to take the call. Mediums often have the same sort of problem.

The medium's job is to first establish the right person for whom the spirit person – the communicator – has a message, and this is called 'making the link' between the two of them. Sometimes it is very easy: the medium sees or hears the spirit person and is immediately drawn to a particular man or woman in the audience, but at other times it is much harder. For instance, what happens if the medium can describe the communicator perfectly, but is given no indication at all who to go to? In that case the medium has little option but to continue to give information about him or her – possibly a name, or how or when they passed away, or where they lived, or what they did, or what their connection with the person they want to contact is, until the communicator is recognised.

When this sort of situation happens, mediums say that 'Spirit is making them work'. Usually they are successful, and eventually 'find their link', and give the message as normal. However, occasionally, possibly because the connection with the member of the audience was very long ago – even on occasions from schooldays – they don't succeed, and have to 'cut the link,' (give up) and pass on to another communicator.

A variation of this problem can be where the medium describes the communicator, and feels certain that he/ she wants to contact a particular member of the audience, but that person can't understand who the communicator is. If all else fails, and no link is made, the only thing that the medium can do is to 'leave him/ her with the person' and move on to another communicator, just hoping that the person will remember who the original communicator was at a later time.

Some of the strongest evidence of the survival of a personality after the death of the physical body can come in this way. For instance, if the person in the audience goes home and discusses the matter with a family member, often they are told 'Oh, that was ...' – someone whom the person in the audience didn't even know – and the message that came through was really for that other family member.

Let's go back to the problems that a medium may face. Sometimes, when a communicator has been described, several members of the audience can recognise the description, and then the medium has to whittle them down by giving additional information. For instance, just imagine that there are four people who can recognise a description: the medium might then say, 'He was a manual labourer' or 'He smoked a pipe' or 'He lived by a railway line' or 'He loved horse-racing', and after each bit of information ask if all could still understand the description. Inevitably, some will drop out, until hopefully only one is left – the 'link'.

However, sometimes two people are left – a 'double-link' – and the medium can't sort them out. In that case the probable reason is that the message is a spiritual message, and will apply to both of them, as their personal circumstances are similar. For instance, both of them may be in a 'piggy-in-the-middle' situation between two warring family members, and the spiritual message might be identical for both of them: 'Sit back and refuse to take sides, or else you will be drawn into the argument.'

These few instances show how difficult it can be for mediums to 'find their link', and how those who can do so in public every time, do such a wonderful job.

How does a medium prepare for a demonstration?
Before going onto the platform, mediums will spend a little time in private meditation. The object of this period is to release all connections with their everyday concerns, and

clear their mind of all personal distractions, so they can focus on the job in hand – which is giving messages. They call in the spirit guides, and ask that all evidence which they give shall be clear, true and accurate. They will already have put protection round themselves, usually in their morning meditation, but they may wish to repeat the protection, so there will no possibility of being influenced by negative entities.

What is the difference between 'a message' and 'a reading'?

Both are essentially the same thing, a communication between a spirit person and someone on Earth. The only differences lie in minor details.

The first one is that a message is given in public, either in a church service or in a demonstration. It is usually fairly short – the ideal time is about five minutes, which is enough for the member of the congregation or audience to identify the communicator and to receive what the communicator has to say. Some inexperienced mediums 'hang on to their link', and continue giving more and more information about the communicator, which might be fine for the recipient, but is rather boring for the rest of the people in the congregation or audience.

However, some people want a more private session, and so ask for a reading with a medium. There are two possibilities: sometimes they just want a single question answered, possibly about their own spiritual development and gifts or talents; at other times they want a more in-depth reading, such as being given information to prove that a dear-departed loved one still exists. In that case, the longer the reading is, and the more personal information which can be given, the better the client is pleased.

To cater for the former, many Spiritualist centres provide an 'on-the-night, one-to-one' service, where any member of the congregation or audience can have a five or ten minute reading with a medium for a nominal sum of money, possibly £3 to £5.

Where the latter is required, members have to make their own private arrangements with a medium, and pay whatever the going rate for mediums is in that area. This may be anything between £15 for a 30-minute reading up to £60 or more for an hour. Many Spiritualist churches are happy to arrange sittings with either visiting mediums or local mediums who are members of the church, and most centres – although not usually doing the arrangements themselves – will provide a list of reputable mediums that they can recommend.

Although most mediums still work 'face-to-face' with clients, many now give telephone readings, and this is usual where a medium is contacted via a magazine advertisement or on the internet. In these cases, the medium establishes 'the link' through hearing the voice of the client. Where the client is already known to the medium, and so it is easy to establish the link, some mediums will even send readings by email, although this is not general practice, as it involves a lot of typing.

What are the Different Types of Mediumship?

We have already mentioned the three main types of mediumship, clairvoyance, clairaudience and clairsentience, but there are many other types, some of which are so rare that even many long-term Spiritualists have never heard of them. Let us start with the one which everyone has heard of which is healing. Healing is practised in all Spiritualist churches and centres and is normally free, although sometimes 'free-will donations' are suggested. There are also independent healers who charge for their services, but these usually work in their own home or environment. Some healers who normally work in churches or centres also accept patients for free consultations within their own homes.

How does a healing medium work?

Whether or not new patients are seen in a church, a centre or at home, the initial approach is the same. A little time is spent putting them at ease, asking them if they have had healing before, giving an explanation of how healing works, and explaining that the healing energies are from doctors in spirit, and are merely passed through the healer, not from the healer personally. The patients are then told to relax completely, and the session begins.

Mediums will then 'call in' the healing guides, at the same time placing their hands on the shoulders or the head, and will be guided to where their hands need to go: the healing goes to the cause of the problem, not necessarily where the pain is. Most healers are fully conscious during the healing, but a few rare ones work while in trance. The hands remain on the patient for as long as it takes for the healing to be effective, and the guide decides when to take them off or to move them to another part of the body. It must be explained to the patient that the healing will not necessarily cure the condition, but it always helps.

Not all healers work in the same way; for example, some don't need to touch the patient at all. Whenever necessary, people are advised to also seek a doctor's opinion.

One specialist form of healing is known as 'psychic surgery'. This is done in trance conditions, and healers allow their spirit surgeon guide to take control and operate through them. Psychic surgeons do some amazing work, usually without any instruments at all and there have been instances where tumours have been removed, confirmed by later X-rays of the affected area.

One of the most famous of all psychic surgeons is 'John of God', who practises in a small town in Brazil. Millions of people have travelled from all over the world to him for healing, and some have been so amazed by their experiences that, in gratitude, they have stayed on at his centre as volunteers to help with the logistics of dealing with the thousands of sufferers who still go there every year.

However, there have been many people who are totally sceptical of his supposed gifts, and have denounced him as a complete charlatan. 'The jury is still out' on whether he is genuine or a fake, but after almost forty years of practice, with thousands of documented healings, some credence must be given to his powers. There are a large number of websites about 'John of God': put his name into Google and take your pick.

However, without resorting to visiting famous names, I myself have been a witness to one amazing healing, which may possibly come under the heading of 'psychic surgery'. In the first Spiritualist church I ever attended, there was a weekly healing evening, during which members of the public could come and ask for free healing for a variety of complaints. One lady came in who had a huge lump on her neck – possibly a goitre or some such condition. Our chief healer went to her, put her hands round her neck, and stayed there for about ten minutes in prayer. At the end of the time, she took her hands away – and the lump had disappeared. Physically, it was impossible, but yet it happened, and I witnessed it.

Healers do not normally speak during the session, but tell the patient what they have felt afterwards. However, some clairvoyant healers do make comments while they are healing, and we have one amazing trance healer friend whose spirit guide – a Chinaman – himself speaks to the patient while he is doing the healing.

What is a healing cure?

While we are speaking of healing, we must ask, 'What is a healing 'cure'? In the minds of most people, the word 'cure' means the removal of the disease, and the complete restoration to full health of the patient, but what about those who are at the end of a long life, and are suffering a terminal illness, as well as having all the problems associated with old age? Would the removal of the terminal illness be a blessing for them, or a curse?

As most human beings can't imagine any sort of existence after the death of the physical body, the normal instinct is to try to prolong life as much as possible. This leads to many of the hideous situations where people with appalling physical illnesses – Motor Neurone Disease and the like – are desperate to have their life ended by euthanasia, and yet are forbidden to by the law and by well-meaning religious people who say that 'only God can take away life.' It's no wonder that most people say 'You wouldn't let even an animal suffer like that, you would put it out of its misery'. Perhaps as human beings we should realise that all of us come to this Earth to learn lessons, and when those lessons have been learned we are allowed to 'go home'.

What are the Different Types of Mediumship?

I once heard a very touching story about a healer who had visited a terminally ill patient for a long time, but one day, when he went to see him, he found out from relatives that the man had collapsed and died. However, he had left a little letter behind, which said simply, 'Thank you for all you're healing over the years: I am now cured.'

Inspirational speaking

This is where mediums either 'hear' or 'sense' their spiritual guide giving information, and then relay that information to either an audience or to a private client. Sometimes only ideas are put into the mind of mediums, and they are stimulated to speak on that subject out of their own knowledge, at other times new information is given. This happens very often in evangelical Christian churches, where they are known as 'charismatic' speakers, (although, of course, no-one would ever admit that they are actually mediums.)

Channelling

One of the spiritual gifts and talents which is little known outside Spiritualism is that of 'channelling'. Channelling is another form of either clairaudience or clairsentience, similar to inspirational speaking, but in this case mediums allow the guide to 'take over' their voice-box and speak through them, usually in a completely different voice.

Some mediums are fully aware of what is going on while the information is being transmitted – what is normally called 'semi-trance' – but others are 'taken over' completely by their guide, and have no knowledge at all of what is happening, until they are told at the end of the session. This is called 'full trance'.

In my case, when I stand up to give a channelled message, I am in semi-trance: I feel that I am standing behind myself, listening to what I am saying. I have no control at all over the content of what is being said, although sometimes I make little comments to myself about it, such as, 'That's an interesting way of putting it: I must remember that.', or 'I had never thought of that before.'

A variation of this gift is where the medium writes the information down as he/ she receives it, and this is in fact how I wrote one of my books: I sensed the information as it was being given to me and then typed it immediately into the computer.

Channelled words can be on any subject, but are often given as comfort when people are in a time of great stress. One Christmas, I was asked to help a lady who had just lost a beloved mother, and was grieving deeply. I asked my channelling guide for something which could help her, and was given some beautiful words of comfort for her, which I will reproduce. (The passage is fairly long, but I hope that you will agree that it is worthwhile printing it out in full).

'Beloved child, I am asked by my instrument to give you a few words on which you can meditate at this time in your life.

Christmas is a time of joy, when most people feel the expression, on a spiritual level, of the original Love which was manifest in the birth of that small baby in a manger some two thousand years ago. At this time all try to express their love to others by the giving of presents and by gathering together socially; they usually celebrate also by treating themselves to luxuries which they would not normally be able – or willing – to indulge in at other times of the year.

From the spiritual point of view this is also the time when those who have made their transition to this side of life draw near to those whom they have left in your world: the vibrant energy of Love which pervades everything at this time acts like a magnet to attract them to be with their loved ones once more. Indeed, they are never more than a thought away, as in this dimension original thought and subsequent action are instantaneous, so all that is needed by them is the thought of

What are the Different Types of Mediumship?

being with you, and they are there instantly.

One thing which is not yet clearly understood by human beings is that everything in Creation is made up of the same 'material' – and this 'material' can best be described in your terms as 'Love'. This was the original force which produced the act of Creation itself, and it is still the most potent force in the Universe. Love can be expressed in many different ways, and if you meditate on the word itself you will be amazed at the many manifestations of it in daily life. But the most amazing thing of all is that all such manifestations are part of the same basic energy: by performing an act of Love in one form, you are in effect showing it in all of its forms. By tending a sick animal or an ailing plant, by comforting a sick child or helping an aged person to cross the road, you are expressing Love in just as active a way as if you were consoling a bereaved person or even locked in the most intimate physical embrace with your soul mate.

When you realise that the love which you felt for your beloved mother while she was still on the earth plane still exists – you did not stop loving her once she was no longer in the physical body, did you. - and that the spiritual communion between you still carries on, although the physical expression of it is no longer possible, then it could help you to start to enter into a new and wonderful phase of your life. Your mother has finished the tasks – and learnt the lessons – for which she originally came into this incarnation, and so she was allowed to return 'home'. But that does not mean that her association with you has ceased: far from it. It means that she is now able to work with you in ways which were not possible during her earthly life, helping, inspiring, supporting and suggesting new things which you can do together – so that you no longer work as two separate individuals, but you can work as one.

When you rise from your bed each morning, send out a silent thought to ask her what you are going to do together during the day, and tell her of your own current intentions.

73

You may sometimes find that thoughts come into your head which will modify your programme. Then, whatever you are doing, from time to time talk to her and include her in what is happening, just as you might once have done while she was still by your side. Finally, at the end of the day, send out your thoughts once more thanking her for being with you and helping you, and expressing your love in whatever way you wish – and feel the Love which she is able to send to you.

Now let us put this into a practical perspective: as I have said above, each act of Love that you do, however small and apparently insignificant, is an act which adds to – and is sanctified by – the absolute eternal Love. Therefore whatever you do to help others in any way – not forgetting the plant and animal kingdoms – do it out of your love for your beloved mother. Dedicate it to her, and feel the Love which she expresses in return. This will mean that your life will take on a completely new meaning, as every little action will have the potential of showing your love for your mother and of binding you together far more closely than you were ever bound during her physical life. This may seem impossible to you at the moment, but once you have experienced it you will realise that it is true.

Let me finally add a few words which have an even deeper meaning: as you know, it is a devastating experience to have to sit and watch a loved one suffering, whether that suffering is mental, emotional or physical, and to know that you are powerless to do anything to help him or her. But have you considered that that is what your loved ones on this side of life are experiencing when they watch you grieving? They know that there is no need for continued grief, although they realise that sorrow and the pouring out of tears are an essential part of the healing process for a time after bereavement. So it is of great benefit to them when the loved ones still on the Earth plane finally accept that the 'dear departed' still exist, and get on with their life. Moreover, those 'dear departed' exist in a state which is infinitely more desirable than the one in which they were while in their earthly life. Remember that no-one who is able to communicate through a medium ever says that they would like to be back in their earthly life – because they wouldn't.

I hope that these few reflections may provide help and comfort to you at what is still a difficult time of your year.'

* * *

It is interesting to note that my guides call me their 'instrument', as I am allowing myself to be used by them, in the same way as a musician will use a musical instrument, and this is something which all mediums are quite used to, although non-mediums might find it strange.

Finally, these words have been passed on to many other people who have been bereaved, and who have found them comforting. Should you know anyone who is grieving deeply, it may be a kindness to show them this little passage to see if it can also help them. (They would have to change the word 'Mother' in the text to the name of the dear-departed relative, and possibly change 'she' and 'her' to 'he' and 'him').

What are 'rescue circles'?

I have spoken earlier about what normally happens to those who pass over at the end of a period of illness, and who go straight 'into the Light'. Now is the time to think about those who, for one reason or other, don't.

Apart from those who are either 'in Limbo' or 'in Hell', there are many who pass over who do not know what has happened to them. For instance, if someone is walking down a street during a storm, and a tile falls off a roof onto their head, they could 'die' immediately, but not know that they are 'dead', (which of course they aren't – it is only the physical body which is dead.) So in that case they would walk about, and try to understand what is going on round them, without success. Nobody would listen to what they say any more, or pay any attention to them whatsoever, other people would use their belongings, or possibly live in their house, and nothing would make any sense at all.

Another scenario is where the people know that they are 'dead', but don't know what to do about it, and are waiting for someone to tell them what to do. A Spiritualist medium friend once told me a little story which would be very amusing if it weren't so desperately tragic. She said that she once went on holiday to Malta, and – seeing a funeral procession – decided to follow them and go into the church to the service.

Normally, in any funeral ceremony, whether religious or not, as well as the living friends and relatives of the deceased, who come to 'pay their respects', there are also all the friends and loved ones from 'the other side of life' who gather to welcome the deceased 'back home'. However, in this church she was amazed to find that none of the departed loved ones of the deceased were there – there was a complete lack of any spirit beings at all. So, curious to find out why this was, she went – psychically – into the crypt, where she saw a group of departed personalities gathered round one who had obviously been a parish priest. When she asked them why they were still there, the priest said that they were all dead, and so had to stay there.

She told them that they were now free to 'go into the Light' and urged them to move on, but they said that they were afraid to, as they didn't know what to do, and they didn't know where to go. She explained that they had only to look for, and then walk into 'the Light' and they would then be looked after, but they conferred for a while, and then the priest said that they had decided that they had better stay where they were until the Archbishop came along and told them what to do. (Hopefully, when he eventually did arrive, he was a bit more knowledgeable than the priest was.)

What are the Different Types of Mediumship?

As an aside here, almost sixty years ago I personally spent two years living in Malta, and became so sickened by the way that the Maltese Catholic Church dominated the population that I became almost an atheist. The hierarchy there considered that their form of Catholicism was superior to Roman Catholicism, as St. Paul was shipwrecked on the island and made converts there before going on to Rome. Maltese Catholicism was a strange mixture of orthodoxy and traditional local beliefs about the Devil – such as the idea that he is frightened by firework 'bangers' – and the population was ruthlessly controlled through the local priests. If they themselves know so little about what happens after the death of the physical body it is easy to see why the priest in the story above was so afraid to move on. (In fact, it was the classic case of the blind leading the blind.

In all of the above scenarios, the personalities, although departed from this life, have not yet reached the next life – the 'other side of life' – and so need help, and since the greatest way of showing Love – and worshipping God – is by service to others, some advanced Spiritualists sit in special 'rescue circles' to help to move them on into the Light.

In these circles, after strong protection has been put around all of the members, to shut out all possible negative entities who might want to intervene, the members all send out their thoughts of Love to try to pick up the vibrations of those needing help: for this purpose I shall call them 'lost souls'. When members have made contact with any one of these, they tell the rest of the sitters so that they also can try to tune in to the same vibration to see if they can pick up any more, after which they direct the lost soul towards the Light.

Usually, when an initial link has been made with one lost soul, it is found that there are a lot more of them who are on the same vibration who can be helped, and very often – once the first one has been directed towards the Light – the rest will follow like sheep, glad that something has at last happened to show them what to do. In one amazing circle we conducted, one of the members tuned in to someone who must have been killed in a large-scale massacre somewhere or other, as there were hundreds of lost souls there, and when that first one was told what to do, and pointed in the right direction, he attracted others, who followed him, and eventually they all queued up in a very long line and followed into the Light.

Elsewhere I mention that time, as we understand it, does not exist out of our world, so sometimes we find that the lost souls have been in that situation, waiting to be directed, for many hundreds of years. In fact, on one memorable occasion we contacted a whole platoon of Roman soldiers, several dozen strong, who had obviously all been killed in some epic battle two thousand years ago, and had stayed together since. Once we explained to the centurion what to do, they all formed up in ranks and marched off quite happily into the Light.

Although rescue circles can be quite hard work emotionally, from a spiritual point of view they provide some of the most interesting and fulfilling work that anyone can possibly do in Spiritualism.

Clearance

Sometimes, personalities stay close to the place where the physical body died, either because they have a strong sentimental attachment to that place or because the circumstances of their death – for instance, a murder – have tied them to it emotionally. In these cases, if they know how to move on but don't want to, and if they are not causing any problem for the current occupiers of the premises, there is nothing much to do. All that one needs to do is to contact them, find out why they are still there, and report back to the current occupiers, to put their mind at rest.

However, there are cases of personalities who find it interesting to play tricks on the occupiers, possibly moving or hiding things, banging doors, or appearing to – and frightening – people. Some, who 'died' long ago, find all the new types of electrical apparatus fascinating, and experiment by switching things on and off. Whatever the situation, if they are causing trouble, after a while the place gets a reputation for being 'haunted', and the 'ghosts' who are doing the haunting have to be moved on. This must be done by mediums who are not only qualified but also experienced in this kind of work. I myself have been present during many clearances, although – as I am not a clairvoyant medium – I have never conducted one personally.

Sometimes the task is very easy: if they are causing trouble because they are merely confused, and don't know what to do, it is a simple case of Rescue: they are told to look round until they see the Light, and then walk towards it. If, however, they refuse to move on, then it is a case of exorcism. The medium has a spiritual battle with the 'ghost', and usually wins. Light will always prevail against Darkness. In the exceptional case of the 'ghost' proving too strong – or too stubborn – to be moved, the Lord Michael – Archangel Michael – is called in to sort out the situation, and he personally escorts the offender into the Light.

Lord Michael's services are always called on where there is a case involving 'fallen angels'. These are dealt with normally only by the highest level of medium, ordained ministers, as there are special techniques involved. It is of little value banishing a harmful entity from one place, if the only effect is to move it on to another, so what happens is that Lord Michael escorts the entity back to its proper 'home' – the second dimension – and seals it in there, so that it can never trouble humanity again.

Precognition

This literally means 'before-knowing', or to use a more common everyday word, forecasting. Throughout history mankind has tried to find out what is going to happen in the future, and many ways of doing so have been created. Most start with a period of observation, which is then followed by forming a theory about what is happening. This is followed by testing the theory, and if necessary refining it and re-testing, until eventually it is fairly certain that the theory is correct. In science, this is normally called 'the scientific method', and originally the science of astronomy started as astrology, when – thousands of years ago – people in the Middle East tried to work out the influence of the sun, moon and planets on events in human life, and had to make a detailed study of the night sky in order to do it. These days, scientists decry and deride astrology, despite it having been the inspiration for astronomy, but it is, of course, still widely practised.

However, a far less controversial method of forecasting is practised by those who live an outdoor life, gardeners, shepherds, farmers and the like. Since their livelihood depends on the weather, the seasons, the best times to sow seeds or plants, etc., most of them develop a sixth-sense of forecasting what is likely to happen to the weather in the future, and there have been many famous weather predictors who have had no sophisticated tools at all apart from their own personal knowledge and their powers of observation. Moreover, the long-term forecasts of many of them have often in the past proved more accurate than those of the professional weather forecasters and their computers.

In Judaism and Christianity, divination, trying to find out what lies ahead, was always denounced – unless it was done by established prophets, many of whom forecast the future birth of the Master Jesus. However, he himself also made forecasts about the future, one of which was the destruction of the Temple in Jerusalem.

As an aside here, it is interesting that Christians still denounce astrology, and yet one of the cornerstones of the Christmas tradition is the story of the Magi, the wise men, visiting the new-born baby, guided by the star. (The 'Magoi' were a Zoroastrian sect of astrologer-priests who were well-versed in interpreting the movements of various heavenly bodies, and they had interpreted the appearance of the 'star' – more probably a conjunction of planets – as announcing the birth of a great king.)

The book of the Revelation is based round the prophetic visions of St. John, and many fundamentalist Christians see us now being in the 'End Times', facing Armageddon, and the final victory of righteousness in the war between Good and Evil.

Away from such extreme beliefs, many people over the centuries have made prophetic forecasts: the most famous one was Nostradamus (1503-1566), but others have included Mother Shipton, (1488-1561), Edgar Cayce, (1877-1946) and the more recent Bulgarian seeress Baba Vanga, who made some amazing predictions before her death in 1996, some of which refer to present events in the Middle East and Europe. All of those mentioned above are worth looking up on the internet.

Quite apart from such famous people, many ordinary men and women have precognition, which in common language is called 'intuition' or 'premonition'. (Premonition literally means 'before-warning'.) However, most mediums have this to a much heightened degree.

This is why many people consult mediums: they are curious about the future. They want to know whether they are going to meet the man/ woman of their dreams, or have children, or win the Lottery, and other such matters – and of course there are plenty of mediums who are happy to satisfy their curiosity in private readings. Most of these mediums are genuine, with great psychic gifts, but inevitably, where there is money to be made, there will always be charlatans, and this is why I have suggested that you choose a private medium only by word-of-mouth recommendation or by reference from a Spiritualist church or centre.

However, most Spiritualist mediums scorn mediums who specialise in answering questions like those above, and dismiss them as 'fortune-tellers'. They prefer to use their own gifts to help, comfort and console or encourage people who are seeking spiritual answers to the current life situations in which they find themselves, and although you will find occasional references to the future in Spiritualist messages they will not be the main part of the message.

Dreams
All people have dreams from time to time, but very few dreams seem to have any meaning to the average person, although there are some psychologists who specialise in dream interpretation – and in fact have written books on the subject. There are also many mediums who have a special form of precognition which shows itself through dreams, and can 'foresee' world events. For instance, there were hundreds of people who claimed to have 'seen' the death of Princess Diana – but of course, those claims were made after the event, so they couldn't be verified.

However, for anyone who believes that they might have the gift, there is a very simple way of proving it. Keep a 'dream diary'.

A dream diary is a little notebook which is kept by the bedside, and into which the date and contents of the dream are entered. However, there are some problems. One is that we all tend to forget dreams very quickly – hence the need to make a note of them – and very often when we wake up in the morning we remember that we had a dream, but we forget what it was all about. So it is necessary to make a note as soon as you wake up after the dream – and if this is in the middle of the night, so be it. The second problem is that writing a lengthy résumé of the content in the middle of the night could well stop you getting back to sleep afterwards.

So possibly the ideal answer is to keep a little notepad by the side of the bed, and make a brief note in it of main keywords to act as reminders – e.g. night, house, flash, stairs, or whatever is appropriate – immediately after the dream, and then write it up more fully in the main diary when you wake up in the morning. With practice, you can condition your mind to always waking up after you have had a dream and then to going to sleep afterwards.

Leave a space of a few lines at the end of the write-up for future insertions.

Now if – or let's be positive, when – something happens which you can interpret as having been forecast in your dream, go back to the original entry and make a note of the event, the date and the length of time since you had the dream. This will give you a basic 'benchmark' to judge future dreams by. Then, when you have a particularly vivid dream in future, which seems to be a warning of some sort, add your 'benchmark' number of days or weeks to the current date and note it in your calendar as a possible time when the thing will happen. Make sure that you write up your diary every time that you have a dream: the fuller the description the more useful it will eventually be.

If you really do have the spiritual gift, then you should fairly quickly establish not only when to expect something to happen, but also precisely what it could be. Many people who have dreams find that instead of just being recognisable events, the dreams contain a lot of strange situations which can only be some sort of symbols, and so at a later date, when reading through your dream diary, you could start to understand the meaning of those symbols, and how they work out in practice.

Psychometry

Psychometry – two Greek words meaning 'soul measurement' – is practised by a medium who holds a personal possession belonging to a client, and then draws from it information about the client or the previous owner of the article. This is an advanced form of clairsentience. It is based on the fact that different levels of vibrations are able to exist at the same time in any one article.

A very good analogy for this is to think of a sponge, containing water within the little spaces inside. When the sponge is squeezed, the water is expressed. In the same way, the finer vibrations of the present or previous owners can enter into the more solid material of the article and remain there until 'expressed' by the medium.

Special clairsentience

There are some mediums who are psychometrists, but who use their gifts in a special way, through the use of special items. The ones most used are either flowers or ribbons, so the respective gifts are called 'flower clairsentience' and 'ribbon reading'.

Let us say something about the science behind these gifts. (There is a more detailed study of this in the last chapter of the book, 'The scientific background', but let us sketch out the general idea here.)

Everything in existence consists of vibrations, and finer vibrations can exist within coarser vibrations. I have given a simple practical example above, a sponge – coarse vibrations – which can contain within itself water– finer vibrations. The water is able to enter the holes in the sponge and be stored there. In the same way, the vibrations of our own personality are very fine, and can be – and are – absorbed into the 'holes' of everything physical that we touch.

Therefore, by holding an item for a short length of time, we are infusing that item with some of our own vibrations, and all that the flower or ribbon reader is doing is the equivalent of psychically 'squeezing' the flower or ribbon in order to 'sense' our vibrations.

What are the Different Types of Mediumship?

When a flower demonstration is done, all members of the audience are asked to bring a flower, and all the flowers are put onto a tray in front of the medium, who picks one out at random and then gives a 'psychic' reading on the character of the person who brought it. After that, the medium asks who has brought the flower, and may or may not end by giving that person a bit of advice. In one demonstration which I saw the amusing message was, 'Next time, bring your own flower, and don't steal one from someone else's garden.'

Ribbon readings are slightly different. The medium will have a 'ribbon-stick' – a piece of wood with as many as sixty ribbons of different colours on it, and will offer it to members of the audience to choose three colours. From experience, the medium will know that each colour vibration has a certain meaning, and so a message can be given to those members, which gives advice about situations in their personal circumstances at the time.

To refer back to what I have just said, about the vibrations of our own personality entering objects which we touch, that raises interesting questions about second-hand shops, and particularly charity shops which sell clothing. If we buy something as personal as clothes which others have worn, there is a fair chance that we will start to pick up some of the vibrations of the previous owners when we are wearing them. In most cases, it won't make any difference at all, but if the new owner happens to be particularly psychic, he/ she could start to sense the physical or mental conditions of the previous owner, and feel uncomfortable wearing the item – particularly if the previous owner is now 'dead'. So if this sort of thing happens to you, the short answer is, 'Get rid of the item.'

To quote a personal example of this, due to special circumstances, for some time the weekly demonstrations which we attended had to be held in a Charity shop and the audience was seated in between rows of second-hand clothes and personal items. However, we soon found that we were picking up some very disturbing vibrations, which had to be cleared before the medium could start working, and as new clothes and bric-a-brac were being brought in every day, this clearance had to be repeated quite often. We finally decided that it wasn't a good place to hold demonstrations, and moved on to more suitable premises.

Aura reading

Another special kind of medium is an aura reader. He/ she is clairvoyant, but 'sees' the aura – energy field – around the client, and is able to interpret the different colours which are in the aura to give clients information, particularly about health or emotional conditions around them. It is rare to find a medium doing only aura reading by itself in a demonstration or in a service, but many mediums incorporate a bit of aura reading in their normal work. If anyone wishes to read more about the aura, look in the section on 'Kirlian photography' at the end of the book.

Psychic art

This is a lesser-known gift, which is never seen and demonstrated during a church service, but it is still seen from time to time in demonstrations in centres. Once mediums have 'called in' the artist guides, they allow them to take complete control of their hands, and either draw or paint a portrait of a spirit personality who is a loved one of someone in the audience. While they are doing so, mediums will usually give a running commentary of what they sense about the communicator, what sort of characteristics or interests he/ she had, etc. so that the audience have both a word picture as well as a physical picture. Sometimes, two mediums will work together during a demonstration: one gives normal messages while the psychic artist is concentrating on working on the picture, free from interference. Finally, the artistic medium asks who can understand the descriptions, and whoever does – there is rarely more than one person – is given the drawing as a souvenir.

The reason why it is never seen in a service, is that the part of a service devoted to clairvoyance is not usually longer than half an hour, and since it takes anything up to twenty minutes to do a full piece of psychic art, there is not really enough time to fit in more than one in the time available However, the normal demonstration in a centre lasts for an hour, and so three or sometimes even four can easily be done in that time.

A variation of this gift is where a medium sits alone, calls in the guide, and then paints a spirit picture. Some mediums develop this to such an extent that they give private sittings, during which they paint the portrait of the main guide of the client. I had a friend who was a brilliant psychic artist who, before a service, would paint several psychic portraits which would be the loved ones of members of the audience that evening, and then give them out at the demonstration. Not only that, but if the members hadn't arrived at the place yet, he would put the portraits on the chairs they would be sitting on. A rare gift indeed.

Musical composition

It is well known that there are historical cases of people who have showed musical ability at a very early age, for instance Mozart, who learned to play the piano at the age of four, and composed his first symphony when only eight. What is less known is that there are also cases of people who have written musical compositions, which they claim was inspired by the spirits of past great musical composers. One of these was the late Rosemary Brown, who claimed to have written works inspired by any one of fifteen such composers. Some musical experts studied her work and agreed that there were definite resemblances to the style of the composers claimed, although others violently disagreed. As there is no way of verifying these claims, perhaps one should view them with caution, but since it is certainly not impossible for the personality of a former musical master to work with a budding composer, perhaps we may be surprised one day.

A late 19th Century French medium, George Aubert, had no interest whatsoever in music, and yet when in trance was able to play flawlessly highly technical piano pieces in the style of various composers. In laboratory experiments he performed perfectly, even when all efforts were made to distract him, such as playing two different, and very loud, pieces of music into different ears while he was performing, and sticking pins into his hands during his performances.

Automatic writing

Once more, mediums 'call in' the writing guide, and then relax, with a pencil in their non-writing hand. They then 'switch off' their attention by concentrating on something completely different, and allow the writing guide to use their hand to produce written information. When such information is studied, it is often found that it is about something which is totally outside the current conscious knowledge of the medium, and as further proof, it has been known that the final product is script written backwards, so that it can be read only by using a mirror.

Physical mediums

There are some mediums who have such rare gifts that ordinary Spiritualists have very little chance of ever witnessing demonstrations of them. The gifts all produce 'physical' results, things which can be experienced with our normal five senses, and so the mediums who have these gifts are called 'physical mediums'.

Some of these gifts involve using energy in ways that scientists would say are 'physically impossible', and yet they happen. I myself have taken part in one such experiment, which is generally known as 'table-moving'.

Table-moving

In one home circle which we had, there were about six of us in the group, and we decided to try 'table moving'. Each of us placed one finger under a table, and concentrated to see if, by the power of thought alone, we could get it to lift up – and we were successful. It could be said that six people could easily lift a table, even with only one finger each, but if they did then at least they would show some signs of strain – and no-one felt any strain at all.

However, the sequel could not be faked: we sat one of the members of the group on a chair, and four of us lifted her up to a height of about three feet by the same method. It sounds ridiculous, but it happened.

Transfiguration

Transfiguration mediums really demonstrate two different skills at the same time. In a demonstration, they channel the voice of a spirit personality, but also allow that personality to re-mould the shape of their own face, so that the members of the audience see and hear the person as they were in life. I have only ever seen one example of this during my whole life as a Spiritualist, but that demonstration was certainly very dramatic, with about six different changes of face and voice during the evening. It was particularly evidential when the medium, who was a well-built man with a definite masculine voice, 'brought through' a tiny woman, who had a tiny feminine voice.

Materialisation

This is the 'classical' activity in séances which was relatively common in Victorian times, but is virtually unheard of today. It involved mediums producing 'ectoplasm' from their own body, which was then moulded by unseen hands into the physical forms of departed loved ones of the members who were sitting in the room at that time. Ectoplasm is a sort of rubbery substance, which can be touched and held, and those who have had the opportunity to hold it say that it feels 'warm and flesh-like.' I have one such friend, a very old lady who – twenty years ago – was involved in some psychic experiments which included materialisation and she has confirmed that it was all genuine.

One of the problems of ectoplasm is that it is very light-sensitive, almost like a photographic film, and cannot be produced except in the dark, or at most, in very dim red light. (This is what gave rise to all the stories of Spiritualists dabbling in necromancy, and calling up the Devil.)

In typical materialisations, mediums and their clothing are examined thoroughly to make sure that nothing is being hidden which could produce the expected effects, and then they are seated in a cabinet, lined with black, to keep out all light. Their hands and feet are securely tied to the chair, so that they cannot move, and then a black curtain is drawn to seal the cabinet. After a short while, a white, misty cloud is seen seeping round and under the edges of the curtain, and this cloud solidifies and takes the shape of a human being. By this time the eyes of the members present are becoming accustomed to the low light, and as the cloud becomes brighter the features of the communicator become clearer. This spirit form – that of a loved one known to one of the members there – then moves to them, takes their hand, and speaks to them. After a while it retreats back into the cabinet, and is replaced by another.

Since materialisation involves mediums producing ectoplasm from their own body, it is most important that strict discipline is observed during the demonstration. Members of the circle must not move about, unless requested to by the medium's controlling guide, and although in some circumstances photography is permitted, flash photography is definitely forbidden. In the later years of Victorian demonstrations, the curtain was dispensed with, and it was then possible to take photographs of the medium while he or she was working. So now many photographs exist of famous mediums producing ectoplasm, usually from the mouth or nostrils, but most of these photographs were produced by time exposure.

The reason for the strict discipline is that at the end of the session the ectoplasm is slowly absorbed back into the medium's body, and if anything happens to suddenly cause a rapid re-integration back into the body that can cause serious psychic harm to the medium. In fact, when an 'investigator' tried to debunk Alec Harris as a fraud, by throwing his arms round the ectoplasmic form which had materialised, the form dissolved within his arms immediately, leaving a very scared 'investigator'. However, the medium suffered a severe psychic shock, which it was claimed eventually led to his death.

There are many books still available about famous materialisation mediums, such as Alec Harris, Daniel Douglas-Home and Helen Duncan. If you are interested look them up on Google. All had their detractors, and many investigators claimed to have proved that they were fraudulent, and yet many others, who attended their séances, were convinced that they were genuine. As it is said, 'You pays your money and you takes your choice' about what you believe.

Apports

Apports are things which are brought into the circle through the body of the medium, usually from the mouth. An apport can be any one of a number of things, flowers, stones, jewellery, etc. They are produced in full light, after the medium has been scrupulously examined to ensure that nothing is being hidden on the body or in the clothing which could lead to fraud. The late Sai Baba was reputedly an expert in producing apports and giving them to his devotees.

Direct voice

The traditional method of producing 'direct voice' was in a séance in a darkened room, where there would be a 'trumpet' – in reality a small horn – on a table in the centre. After a time, when the eyes of members had become used to the darkened atmosphere, the trumpet would rise from the table and – in mid-air – would circle round the room of its own volition, and would come to rest in front of one of the members there. Then the 'direct voice' of a loved one of that member would be heard, giving him/ her a message. After a time, the message would end, and the trumpet would begin circling again, stopping somewhere else and repeating the procedure, to bring a different 'direct voice' to a different member.

A more modern – late 1900s – form of direct voice was when some sort of instrument was used as a 'voice-box'. This could be something like a reel-to-reel tape recorder, which would be placed on the table, frequently without either a tape or a microphone, and then after a time the 'direct voice' would be heard coming from the instrument.

The late Colin Fry, who was a great clairvoyant medium, was one of the best exponents of 'direct voice' of recent years.

Orbs and electrics

Other manifestations often seen in séances might be the production of spirit orbs – globes of light of various sizes – which dance round the room in mid-air, moving erratically and having the ability to pass through physical objects – e.g. the table – and a bank of lights which flicker on and off in random sequences, while the switches are taped off and can't be used.

What are the Different Types of Mediumship?

Outside the séance room, clairvoyant mediums often 'see' orbs of light, and one special form of mediumship is a 'psychic photographer'. These people take photos in which either orbs of light or spirit forms can be seen in the final print, although not visible physically. In one amazing photo which I once saw, a medium was shown giving a demonstration, and several orbs – each containing a face – appeared round her.

For those who might be interested in the manifestations experienced in 'physical' séances, it could be of value to look up 'The Scole Experiment' in Google. These are details of a very intensive research project done in Scole, Norfolk, from 1993 to 1998, which itemises many manifestations of the kinds of mediumship I have outlined above. On occasions my old Spiritualist friend was present at demonstrations there, and has vouched for their authenticity.

Powerhouse

This is the least understood of all kinds of mediumship, because it is never seen by anyone, and never sensed by anyone but mediums – and it is sensed by those only when they are working. I came across it purely by chance, but fortunately in my very early days as a Spiritualist, so that I could understand it later on in life.

The aunt of my first wife was a very powerful medium who once worked on the prestigious Marylebone circuit of Spiritualist churches in London. She introduced me to Spiritualism and so was my virtual spiritual mother. Her husband was a rather grumpy old man, who appeared to have no spiritual gifts whatever. He didn't do anything or say anything, he just sat in services. He was about thirty years older than 'Auntie Margaret', and she appeared to hold him in great awe, rather than affection, so one day I asked her what his spiritual gifts were, and she told me that he was a 'powerhouse'. I had never heard this word before, so I quizzed her further, and she told me that certain people, who may not be mediums in the ordinary sense (and may not even be Spiritualists) have the ability to act almost as spiritual generators. Such people, by their very presence, raise the vibrations of the church or centre to such an extent that the powers of the medium who is performing there at the time are greatly enhanced.

He was the only person whom I ever met like that in the Midlands, where I was brought up, but since I have lived in Torquay, in South Devon, I have found out that there are a great number of powerhouses here – possibly why this area can be thought of as the 'capital' of Spiritualism in the UK: there is probably more Spiritualist activity here, and there are more working mediums, than in any other area of the country comparable in size and population. Furthermore, when we get several 'powerhouses' sitting together in a home circle, things really start to buzz.

Russian experiments

Finally, there was a series of very interesting investigations into psychic phenomena by Russia in the 1960s, and an American woman, Sheila Ostrander, wrote a book about them in 1971. This book has had many reprints, and the latest re-issue, from 1999, is still available in paperback for a modest sum from Amazon. A similar book was published in America at the same time. Edited by Martin Ebon, it itemised a number of pieces of psychic research done in Russia and Eastern European states over the previous decade.

Both books mention many investigations into the paranormal gifts of Russian mediums, including one who could move objects purely by the power of thought – telekinesis.

Nina Kulagina (1920-1990) was the most famous medium mentioned. In 1963 she came to the attention of a Russian physiologist and parapsychologist, who conducted tests on her ability to move objects by thought, and for the next twenty years she was tested by many Russian and Western scientists, who were unable to prove that she was not completely genuine.

The books also have many examples of ESP – Extra-Sensory Perception. (Most people use the more modern word of 'telepathy'.) They also have examples of levitation – rising from the ground and floating in the air, defying gravity. In the UK, one of the most famous mediums who could allegedly levitate was a 19th Century Scottish medium, Daniel Douglas-Home.

What is particularly interesting about the Russian experiments is that they were all conducted by Russian scientists under rigorous laboratory conditions, so the findings cannot be questioned as far as their methodology is concerned. Nor are Russians – particularly in the Stalinist era when most were conducted – likely to be swayed by any religious pre-dispositions. All the more reason to accept the validity of the results.

As I said earlier, all of these kinds of mediumship are extremely rare these days. Perhaps we are just far too materialistic or too sceptical, to accept them, but occasionally young mediums who are in training circles show a possibility of being able to develop such gifts. Perhaps trainer mediums ought to be more aware of this, and more ready to develop such potential.

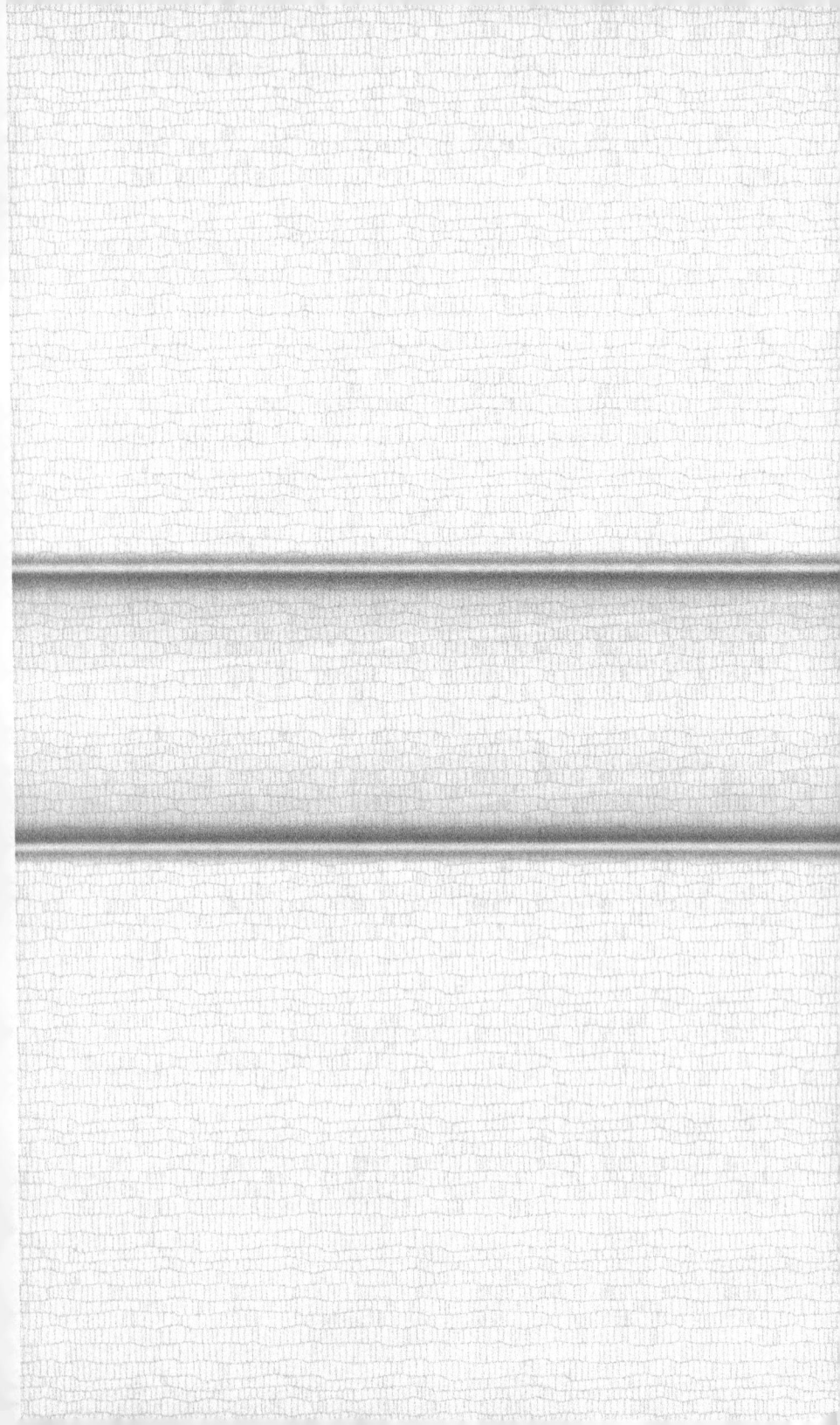

How are Mediums Trained?

Is it possible to learn mediumship by yourself, or do you need to engage a teacher?

Some mediums are what are called 'natural' mediums, which means that they have had all their gifts, of whatever kind they may be, from birth, and even as children have had mediumistic experiences. However, this is very rare, and it is even rarer to find that a natural medium is able to practise in a church or centre without further training. I myself have known many natural mediums over the years, but I have only ever met two who went on to practise straight away.

So the majority of people who have mediumistic potential will attend some course of training or other. However, there is a far greater reason for enrolling on a course rather than trying to do it yourself: and that is the question of safety.

To explain this, just imagine that you have some play equipment in a children's play park, and some of it is potentially dangerous if not used correctly. Would you let a child use the equipment without supervision? Of course you wouldn't. It may be all right, and they may get by without being hurt, but you wouldn't want to take the chance, would you?

However, it is exactly the same sort of scenario if you attempt to develop any spiritual gift without guidance and supervision: you do it at your peril.

Let me give you a personal example: Many years ago I was a member of a healing circle at a church, and we had an open night once a week when members of the public could come along and ask for healing for any medical condition or complaint which was causing them problems. One night a lady was carried in. We were told that one day, three years before, she had visited a neighbour to find that the lady, with some friends, was using a Ouija board. A Ouija board is a primitive psychic device which can be used to contact deceased people, or other non-physical beings.

Although the woman did not take part in the experiment personally – she just stood there and watched – some entity had come through the board and had attached itself to her, and for the next three years she had spent time in several psychiatric hospitals undergoing electric, drug and other therapies to try to drive it out of her – all to no avail.

When she was carried in, her whole body was hideously twisted round, as though she was trying to defend herself from some unseen enemy. Fortunately, that night there were seven healers there – seven is a very powerful spiritual number – and after a great struggle we were able to free her from it, but it served as a lesson to all present not to play with things which you do not understand.

The problem is that unless you are very experienced and well protected spiritually, you may let something in which you don't want. It is the psychic equivalent of leaving your front door open at night: if you do, you might not be able to control whoever – or psychically whatever – takes the opportunity of coming in.

Now although the above possession was the result of the use of an Ouija board, trying to do psychic experiments yourself is a similar sort of situation: you might be all right, but if anything goes wrong and something nasty does come through you almost certainly won't have the knowledge to get rid of it, will you?

What happens on a medium training course?
First of all, you should realise that if you go on a course, it is not a 'quick fix'. The normal length of course is about two years, and during that time you would be attending some centre or church one night a week, on a regular basis, so it is not the sort of thing that you can enter into half-heartedly:

you have to have a certain degree of commitment in the first place, or else just don't bother starting at all.

When you go into the course room, you will find that all the chairs have been set out in a circle. Physically, a circle is stronger than any other shape, and this is also true psychically, as a circle contains the energy far better. No-one is left out, and all those in the circle are psychically connected with each other. In some cases a teaching evening will actually start with those in the circle holding hands during the opening prayer.

There must always be at least one experienced medium in the group, who acts as a Master of Ceremonies, and in a beginners' group there is often more than one, to help to raise and maintain the vibrations. The presiding medium will always open in prayer, and depending on the particular techniques customary in that group will probably explain a way of opening oneself psychically to spiritual influences.

The first thing which you would be taught on the course is how to protect yourself. This is important, as I have mentioned in the previous answer. When you are under training, you are opening yourself psychically, and are therefore allowing yourself to become vulnerable, so the first thing that you would need to do is to learn the various techniques of protection. You won't need these while you are actually in the course room itself, under the control of the teacher, as he/ she will be protecting the whole group, and everyone individually, all the time that the group are sitting – and at the same time keeping a sharp lookout for any possible problems. Nevertheless, you would need to master the techniques yourself before you practise.

There will generally be a meditation at that point. Meditations are usually 'directed' during the early stages of the course. This means that the presiding medium will lead the group through a particular scenario, possibly telling them to visualise certain scenes, and then asking them to imagine themselves on a journey through the landscape visualised. Later on, when the group has got used to meditating, the leader will usually change over to 'free' meditations, when each member goes on their own journey, at their own speed. Instructions for a simple, directed meditation for beginners might typically be as follows:

'Before you start, relax and make yourself comfortable, and then close your eyes.

Now take three deep breaths and put yourself on a country lane, starting to walk along it slowly. Take note of the flowers in the hedgerows and their colours, seeing the wind rustling the trees and hearing the bird-songs. You come to a gate, which you open, go through and close behind you. Finding yourself in a meadow, you walk through it and head for a large tree at the far end.

This is situated by a rambling stream. Sit with your back to the stream, enjoying the peace and listening to the sound of the water. I want you to stay there for ten minutes, and then I will ask you to return – at your own speed – back to where you started, and when you are completely ready to come back to consciousness, slowly wake up. In those ten minutes you may see colours in your third eye in the middle of your forehead, or hear someone speak, perhaps see a face, or a person, or an eye, or sense someone nearby. Or you may sense nothing at all. However, you will return feeling calm and complete'.

* * *

Although this meditation takes up only a few lines of print, in practice it will take the medium several minutes to go through, as he/ she will break it up into small instructions, and allow a minute or so for the sitters to complete each instruction. In that way, without being rushed, the group start to feel that they are there, in the scene, actually doing the actions.

At the end of the meditation each week, each individual will be asked to tell the group what they personally have experienced: they may have 'seen' or 'heard' something, or may have had sensations of various kinds – even smells. Some may have felt something touching their hair, or felt 'cobwebs' on their face. They will be urged to 'give off' – mention – whatever they have experienced, however trivial, and the leader will explain and interpret anything which is not understood.

Finally, the presiding medium will tell the sitters that the meditation can be done at any time, whether in a group or by themselves. However, they will be warned to always remember to bring in their protection before they start, and told that during the time that they are meditating, their spirit guides have the opportunity to help them to become more aware.

Sometimes a member of the group will actually smell the flowers in the hedgerows. The gift of being able to receive psychic smells is called clairolfaction. Occasionally a medium, while giving a message, will pick up a smell, perhaps strong tobacco, after-shave, or a particular kind of perfume, and will mention it as part of the general evidence of the presence of the communicator. However, the experience is not confined to practising mediums: many non-Spiritualists who have been bereaved will occasionally 'smell' – psychically – things which they particularly associate with departed loved ones, and won't be able to understand it. It will be just because the loved ones are around them, and are trying to make them understand that they still exist. (A similar - but rarer - sense is clairgustance, clear tasting.)

All training groups are different, and have their own ways of doing things, but at some time or other during the evening there will probably be a bit of spiritual philosophy, which will explain not just how to do something, but why that something is done

The group will normally do exercises aimed at heightening the psychic sensitivity of the individual, and each time there is a report back to the group on what each member felt.

Finally, the members will be introduced to giving messages, and told to concentrate on another member of the group and say if any particular thoughts come into their mind. If they do, then they would be told to say what they felt, no matter how mundane or stupid they thought that it was. In effect, that is starting to get the group used to communicating with others without shyness. I explained earlier that this is normally called 'working on the psychic', and is a very useful skill to have when a medium hasn't yet picked up any communicator during a demonstration.

It is important that trainee mediums realise that they must 'give off' exactly what they receive, even if they can't understand it. I have heard of mediums 'giving off' some very strange things during demonstrations – for instance sausages, elephants and parrots – and in each case the member of the audience concerned has confirmed that they were evidential to them, even if they sounded ridiculous to everyone else.

There is another reason why the trainees are taught to 'give off' exactly what they receive, and that is to combat the fear of upsetting the recipient of the message. Very often the communicator will want to give the recipient a 'telling off' for doing something which is not in his/ her best interests, and the natural impulse is for the medium to try to hide – or at least soften – the message. That is wrong. Although it is occasionally permissible to change the language that the communicator has used – for instance if it contains swear-words or obscenities – it is not acceptable to change the message otherwise. If the trainee says, 'I don't know how to say this,' then the usual answer will be – a little crudely – 'Say it and sod it.' In other words, pass on exactly what the communicator has said, and if the recipient doesn't like it that is their problem, not yours.

Over the two years, the exercises would get progressively harder and more testing, until by the end of the course each person would be quite at ease standing up and giving a message to anyone who was nominated by the leader.

An example of an advanced exercise is where the course leader asks each member to bring a photo of a family member, in a sealed envelope. The envelopes are given to the leader, who then shuffles them, and gives them out at random. Each recipient then has to give a 'reading' of the character in the photo. Once it is finished, the envelope is opened and the person who brought it is asked to grade the accuracy of the message.

At some time during the course, psychometry is introduced. Each member is asked to put a personal item – a watch, ring, bunch of keys, etc. – onto a pile in the centre of a table, and these are then all mixed up, and each member takes one and gives a psychic reading on its owner. Then the owner of the article rates the reading.

Another exercise might be to blindfold a member and sit someone behind them, and ask the member to analyse the character of that person.

One spiritual gift is that of automatic writing, where the trainee is given a sheet of paper, a pencil and a magazine, asked to put the pencil in their non-writing hand – the left hand for right-handed people and vice-versa – ask their guide to draw something on the paper, and then read the magazine to take their attention away from the pencil for a few minutes. Most people will not get anything legible at all on the paper, but some will find either a drawing or writing on it, which will indicate that they have some potential to do either automatic writing or psychic art.

Another exercise might be where the group is told to write a short poem on any subject of choice. At the end of the given period of time, the efforts are read out, and will show the potential for writing inspirational poetry.

One more might be that the group leader prepares a list of words on cardboard showing different spiritual values – Beauty, Truth, Courage, Compassion, etc. – and these are offered to the members face down for them to pick one. They are then told to speak about that value for a set time – usually two minutes the first time, working up to five later. This will find out whether any member has the possibility of developing inspirational speaking or channelling.

From the above examples, it will be seen that the object of all this training is to prepare trainees to explore what their individual gifts might be, and to get confidence in using those gifts and in interacting with other people. That is another very good reason why it is not possible to learn mediumship by yourself.

Biblical Justification

Are Spiritualism and Christianity mutually exclusive?

The short answer is 'No.', and for a very good reason. Christianity is based on the life of the Master Jesus, and he was the perfect medium. He was in constant communication with the spiritual being that he called 'The Father', which was another way of saying 'God', and the whole of the New Testament is littered with references to spiritual gifts and spiritual phenomena. The most obvious was the gift of healing, which the Master displayed on numerous occasions, but which was also later practised by the disciples. As the Master was the perfect medium, one would expect him to be able to demonstrate all of the gifts, so I shall restrict these few comments to talking about the gifts of the disciples, and the references to spiritual gifts in other parts of the Bible outside the Gospels.

Let us first have a look at spiritual gifts in general. In his first letter to the Corinthians – 1 Corinthians 12.4-11 – St. Paul mentions some of the spiritual gifts. In some of the verses he uses the word 'Lord', in other 'God' and in others 'Spirit', but by implication the words 'Lord', 'God' and 'Spirit' all mean the same thing. That ties in exactly with Spiritualist beliefs, so when they are using their various gifts, and say that they are working 'in Spirit', they are working 'in God'. The only one of the gifts which he mentions which is never used by Spiritualists is 'speaking in tongues'. The reason is that there is no point in speaking in any language which cannot be understood by your audience. In fact, he himself agrees with that view later, and criticises the practice in chapter 14. However, regardless of whatever gifts anyone may have, he emphasises, in chapter 13, that the greatest gift is Love – and once more Spiritualists are in complete agreement.

Clairvoyance and clairaudience

The conversion of Saul is mentioned in Acts 9.3-9. It is interesting in that not only Saul but also those travelling with him 'heard the voice'. Later in the same chapter – vv.10-16 – Ananias also saw a vision and heard a voice.

During the Transfiguration of Jesus, Peter, James and John saw Moses and Elijah with Jesus, and heard a heavenly voice – Matt. 17.1-8 and also Mark 9.2-8, Luke 9.28-36 and 2 Peter 1.16-18.

Two disciples saw and spoke with the Master Jesus on the road to Emmaus – Luke 24.15-35.

The women at the tomb saw and heard an angel who announced the Resurrection of Jesus – Matt. 28.2-7, Mark 16.5-7, and Luke 24.4-8.

Jesus appears to the disciples – Mark 16.14-18 and Luke 24.36-49.

Stephen sees a vision before his death – Acts 7.55-56.

Healing

There are many stories of healing done by the disciples, of which the following references are just a few:

Acts 3.1-8, Acts 5.16, Acts 6.8, Acts 9.33-34, Acts 14.3, and Acts 16.18, Acts 20 10-12, Acts 28.8-9, Luke 9.6, Luke 10.17, Mark 6.13, and Mark 16.20.

Inspirational speaking

The most notable example of this was at Pentecost, where the disciple spoke to each man in his native tongue – Acts 2.4. It is also mentioned in Acts 4.31.

Bestowing of spiritual gifts
The famous prophecy of God giving spiritual gifts in the 'last days', when 'Your young men shall see visions, and your old men dream dreams' is in Acts 2.17. Spiritualists use their 'spiritual gifts' continually.

Dreams
Communication through dreams is also mentioned, as in Matt. 2.13, when Joseph was warned to flee to Egypt, and Matt. 7.19, where Pontius Pilate's wife, after a nightmare, warned him that Jesus was innocent and urged that he should be freed.

* * *

In all, there are more than a hundred examples of spiritual gifts and phenomena in the Bible, both in the Old and New Testaments, so when Spiritualists use one or more of the gifts mentioned it is hard for Christians to condemn them without decrying those who used the same gifts in Biblical times.

Finally, if there is condemnation of any spiritual gift which is exercised and not done within a Christian church, or in the name of the Master Jesus, that denies the validity of any spiritual gifts which are mentioned in the Old Testament. For instance, healing was certainly done by Elijah – 1 Kings 17.17-24 – and Elisha – 2 Kings 4.32-36 – and although they believed in – and worked in – God, they could not be called Christians. So were they 'doing the work of the Devil?'

In the Old Testament there are many accounts of spiritual gifts which were common in Spiritualism in past times, but rarely seen now, such as materialisation – 1 Samuel 28.12-20; direct voice through the use of a trumpet – Exodus 19.19 and 20.18; automatic writing – Exodus 31.18; apports – Numbers 11.31 and levitation – 2 Kings 2.11 – as well as numerous examples of clairvoyance and clairaudience. For instance, in

Biblical Justification

Exodus 3 – re-told in Acts 7.30 – the story of Moses and the burning bush was told. Moses 'saw an angel' and later 'heard the voice of the Lord'. As Moses predated Jesus by hundreds of years, his spiritual gifts could have nothing to do with belief in Jesus.

So historically, at least, Spiritualists are in good company.

Organisation of Spiritualism in the UK

Is there any organisational HQ for Spiritualism, similar to the Vatican in Rome?

No, there is no central hierarchy in Spiritualism which is remotely similar to that of world churches. The major Spiritualist sect in the UK is the Spiritualist National Union, which was set up in 1901 to bring together several separate Spiritualist organisations. It has 350 churches and centres affiliated to it in the United Kingdom. Their main Headquarters and residential teaching centre is at Stansted, Essex. Another teaching organisation is the Spiritualist Association of Great Britain, operating from a building in Belgrave Road, London.

The other major Spiritualist sect is the Greater World, set up in 1931 to promote Christian Spiritualism. It has about 50 churches, and has its HQ in Conway St., London.

However, there are a large number of Spiritualist centres all over the United Kingdom which are not affiliated to any organisation.

Over the years the different factions in Spiritualism have gradually become more estranged – as happens in all religions – and the two main organisations have become more rigid and dogmatic in their own rules. So in 1996 a new Spiritualist organisation was started in order to bring together the different views, and provide a united and more flexible front. It is called the United Spiritualist Fellowship, and has two sides, United Spiritualists and United Spiritual Healers, with its HQ in London. There are currently only a small number of churches and centres affiliated to it.

Finally, the birthplace of the modern Spiritualist movement was in America. It started in the 1840s in a house in Hydesville, New York, where two sisters, Katie and Margaretta Fox, established a system of communication with a murdered peddler who was haunting their house, by doing a series of knockings on walls. It was eventually reported in 1848, and March 31st 1848 is now the official 'birthday' of the Spiritualist movement. The Fox sisters eventually became the world's first mediums to be thoroughly tested and proved as genuine, and over the last 170 years the development of Spiritualism in the United States has steadily grown.

Currently, the most important Spiritualist organisation in the United States is at Lily Dale, in New York. However, there are a large number of independent Spiritualist Associations, many of them organised on a State basis.

The Scientific Background

What is Kirlian photography?

In the early years of the 20th Century there was a Russian, Semyon Davidovich Kirlian, who had achieved local fame in Krasnodar as an electrical engineer and repairer of electrical appliances. He was particular interested in the works of Nicolas Tesla, one of the legendary scientists of his day, whose theories are still being studied today. One day in 1939, Kirlian was watching a patient who was being treated in a high-frequency electrotherapy machine, when he saw a small spark which jumped from the machine onto the patient's skin.

Fascinated by this, he wondered whether it would be possible to photograph it, and experimented by photographing his own hand in a similar machine, and succeeded in producing a photo showing electrical energy – an aura – round his hand.

Over the next ten years, he and his wife did many experiments on the phenomenon, and were able to reproduce the effect without a camera at all, using only photographic film. They then developed a camera which filmed the electrical reaction while it was actually happening. Further experiments on leaves showed that undetected plant diseases could be shown long before they appeared in physical reality.

Continuing to experiment, they turned to photographing the human body, and produced images showing a network of electrical points which corresponded with the traditional acupuncture points and meridians. They then proved that what had been observed in plants about the early prediction of diseases was just as valid in photos of the human body, and after scientific recognition of the technique was granted in 1961, formal Russian state research was done on the concept. It was later reported that many doctors all over Russia were being trained in the use of the photographic technique, and in the study of the colours of the auras produced, as an early diagnostic of disease.

As an aside here, since Kirlian photography proves that there is a system of acupuncture points in the body, which ties up with the ancient Chinese idea of acupuncture 'meridians', and that Chinese system has links to the Indian tradition of energy centres known as 'chakras', then it can be argued that Kirlian photography proves scientifically the existence of chakras.

Finally, as far as Kirlian photography is concerned, there are now very highly developed cameras which are used to show the aura of individuals on a screen in front of them, and also print out copies of that aura, and aura photography prints are available, at a fee, to any members of the public who happen to visit 'Mind, Body and Spirit' exhibitions in various parts of the world.

Some Spiritualists talk of 'chakras'? What are they?

The word 'chakra' is a word in the ancient Sanskrit language, which is the ritual language of Hinduism. It is also known in Buddhism, Jainism and Sikhism. It means 'wheel', and is used to describe the spiritual energy-centres of the body.

We have mentioned the acupuncture meridians of the body, which can be proved to exist by using Kirlian photography, and some mediums who are able to 'see' auras are also aware of parts of the body where different colours in the aura seem to be particularly concentrated. These appear to be in a straight line down the centre of the body, in front of the spine, and traditionally each separate area is associated with a different bodily system, a different gland and a different colour. The areas are called 'chakras' because when a medium views them they appear to be spinning round like little wheels.

Scientists tell us that everything in the universe is composed of atoms, all of which are vibrating, and that each atom contains an enormous amount of energy. So therefore the whole of the universe is composed of energy. Spiritualists also agree that everything is energy, but the view of what spiritual energy is differs from the scientific view. To a Spiritualist, spiritual energy – as well as being a very high level of physical energy at the top of our dimension – is also the Life Force of the organism, and all human beings are as much in need of this Life Force as they are in need of food and drink.

Just as we have physical organs which allow us to take in and digest nourishment in the form of food and drink, so we have spiritual organs which allow us to take in the Life Force, and these spiritual organs are the chakras. In general terms, this Life Force comes in through the Crown chakra, and is then distributed via the other major chakras to the rest of the body. The Crown chakra is situated in the top of the head, and the Life Force enters as white light. In very highly evolved beings, this light is so intense that it can be seen by ordinary men and women as a white haze round the head, from which we get the legends of the Master Jesus and the apostles each having a halo. The Crown chakra is associated with the pineal gland, and with the reception of spiritual communication.

There are seven major chakras, which are the most well-known, but there are also twenty-two minor chakras, all of which have to do with the health of different parts of the body. Four of the most interesting minor chakras are those in the nipples of a woman's breasts and the palms of her hands. These have little to do with the health of the woman herself, but have a great importance for any baby which she might bear. In recent years bottle-feeding has become very common for babies, but the traditional breast-feeding is greatly preferable where possible, as babies are taking in Life Force through the chakras in the nipples at the same time as taking in physical nourishment. They are also taking in the Life Force through the mother's hands, since all babies are continually being picked up and handled.

The main chakras are as follows:

- The white Crown chakra, through which the Life Force is received.
- The Brow chakra is normally seen by clairvoyants as indigo in colour. It is associated with the pituitary gland and receiving spiritual communications.
- The Throat chakra is a sapphire blue in colour. It is associated with the thyroid gland and the metabolism.
- The Heart chakra is emerald green in colour. It is associated with the thymus gland, white blood cells, antibodies and the nervous system.
- The Solar plexus chakra is yellow in colour. It is associated with the pancreas gland and food digestion.
- The Sacral chakra is orange in colour. It is associated with the sex glands.
- The Base chakra is red in colour. It is associated with the adrenal glands, which control responses to stress.

The study of the chakras is a huge subject, and information on them would fill a large book many times the size of this one. We mention them only because one of the specialities of some clairvoyants is Aura Reading, which involves looking closely at the chakras and the colour energies which surround them. For instance, by noting what is happening in the chakras, aura readers can sense what strong emotions their clients are feeling at the time of the reading.

What are 'spiritual vibrations?' Are they any different to 'scientific vibrations?'

Vibrations are vibrations. The only differences between spiritual and scientific ones are the frequencies of each. Scientists tell us that the whole universe is composed of atoms, minute specks of matter so small that they can't be seen with the naked eye. Every atom contains a core, or nucleus, round which spin a number of tiny particles called electrons. The movement of the electrons round the nucleus creates vibrations.

A very simple way to understand – and physically see – vibrations is to think of a guitar. The bottom string is very thick and heavy compared to all the others, and when it is plucked it produces a very low musical note. It vibrates so slowly that it can be seen to be moving backwards and forwards.

The next string up is much finer and lighter, and when plucked produces a higher note. It vibrates much faster, so fast that its movement can hardly be seen at all.

Each string is finer and lighter than the preceding one, and produces a higher note, until the top string – which vibrates so fast that no movement can be seen – produces a very high note.

The number of times that the string vibrates every second is called the frequency of the vibration, and is usually measured in Hertz. So therefore the 'middle C' note on a piano is 256 vibrations per second, or 256 Hertz. When all the strings of the guitar are played at the same time – the guitar is strummed – that produces a musical chord, in which notes of different frequencies are all heard together.

So, to go back to our atoms, since the electrons in each atom are creating vibrations, every atom in the universe is vibrating, and so the universe itself is vibrating, as is everything in it – including us.

Each human being is made up of a lot of different levels of energy, at different frequencies. There is the level of the physical body, a relatively low frequency, then the level of the emotions – a higher frequency. Higher still is the level of the mind, and the highest of all is the level of the spirit, what Christians might call 'the soul'. To differentiate between these different levels, Spiritualists call them 'bodies', so apart from the physical body, every human being has an emotional 'body', a mental 'body' and a spiritual 'body'. As all these 'bodies' exist at the same time within the outer physical frame, but at different frequencies, all have their own electrical force-fields round them.

Although these force-fields cannot normally be seen with the physical eye, they can be photographed with special cameras, and when this is done, it is seen that they form a cloud of light – of different colours – round the body. There appear to be seven different layers within this cloud – the four of which we have spoken – the four 'bodies' – and three intermediate ones, which for the want of a name I shall call 'interfaces' – a good modern computer term.

The cloud of light is usually called the 'aura' of the person, and there are mediums with special gifts of clairvoyance who can actually 'see' auras.

All of these layers extend for different distances from the body, ranging from just half-an-inch for the innermost one to several feet for the outermost. One famous medium has had his outermost – spiritual – layer measured at eighteen feet from his body. I once attended an aura workshop in which we were taught how to measure the distances of the various layers from the body, and that of the leader could be measured at ten feet. However, the normal person's aura extends to only two or three feet.

So when Spiritualists speak of the 'spiritual vibrations' of a person, which is what they are talking about. However, in the same way all spiritual beings from any dimension also have their own vibrations, which can be sensed by many human beings, whether they know that they are mediumistic or not.

What is a dimension?

We have said that everything in our universe is composed of atoms, and that all atoms are vibrating. We have also said that the speed of the vibrations – that is, the number of times that they vibrate in a second, is called their 'frequency'. Human beings are able to detect a small range of frequencies, through their senses of touch, taste, smell, hearing and sight; however, scientists have instruments which can detect and measure the frequencies of many more vibrations, and these instruments can be used to detect even what minerals and gases are present in distant star systems or on other planets.

In our own world, there is a range of frequencies which is far beyond the narrow range of human senses, for instance ultra-sound, X-rays, radio waves, television waves, microwaves and others. I said earlier that when we are trying to understand a difficult idea, it is sometimes useful to compare it to a physical object which is in daily use, and use an analogy. So when trying to understand what a dimension is, we can use the analogy of a thermometer. A thermometer is an instrument which measures temperature, and the normal one usually starts with a temperature of freezing at the bottom of the scale, and boiling at the top, although there are thermometers with a different range, such as those used in cooking for measuring temperatures in jam-making.

Now just imagine that we have a giant instrument something like a thermometer – which I will call a 'vibrometer' – which measures the frequency of vibrations, and it has a scale which can measure all the possible vibrations which exist in our universe. We would call the range of vibrations measured a 'dimension'.

That dimension would be only the frequencies in our universe, but scientists tell us that there are many universes: in fact, one prominent scientist has theorised that there are an infinite number of universes, with totally different ranges of vibrations, and therefore there is an infinite number of different dimensions. However, the current theory which most scientists hold is that there are eleven dimensions which can be mathematically proved to exist.

Spiritual philosophy also says that there are many dimensions, of which two are below ours and up to ten above. So therefore, we are in the 'third dimension'.

What are in the other dimensions?
Spiritual philosophy tells us that the 'first dimension' contains the 'principles' of the basic elements of physical existence, Fire, Earth, Air and Water, plus a fifth mysterious one which has been called 'Ether' or 'Mind' in certain societies. It is possible that it is what scientists speak of when they talk of 'dark energy' – but that remains to be seen.

The 'second dimension' contains the principles of Evil, which are alluded to in various religions. For instance, the Catholic Church talks of 'the Seven Deadly Sins' – although there are far more than seven. This dimension also contains entities which Christianity calls 'fallen angels', and Islam calls 'evil djinns', which are given various names, (Satan, Beelzebub, Lucifer, etc.)

The dimensions above ours are the fourth, which is normally thought of as 'Heaven', and the higher dimensions, all of which are the home to various spiritual entities, archangels, angels, spiritual masters, guides, inspirers and the like, all of whom exist in different dimensions.

According to spiritual philosophy, no entity from any other dimension is ever able to influence human beings unless they are invited in. However, by indulging in any of the 'seven deadly sins', human beings open up pathways from the second dimension into our dimension, and therefore effectively 'invite' harmful entities from that dimension in. Unfortunately, once they are in, they can be very difficult to get rid of.

Do ghosts exist, and if so what are they?

The word 'ghosts' is normally used when the personality of a human being whose physical body has died appears to people who don't know that they have possible mediumistic gifts. As all of us normally fear what we do not understand, and as most people do not understand that the personality of someone still carries on in existence after the death of the physical body, then 'ghosts' are always objects of fear.

We have already said that on the death of the physical body, the personality is released, and normally rises to the vibrational level which is commonly called 'Heaven'. However, as we have said, not all personalities do so, for various reasons. One might be that the personality has a deep emotional attachment to the place where the physical body died; another could be that the circumstances of death were so horrific that they have created a bond between the place of death and the personality. Yet another might be that the death has been so sudden that the personality does not realise that it is 'dead' – which of course is quite true, as it is still in existence, although an existence without a physical body – so it stays where it 'died' until it can work out what to do.

In all of these cases, there is a likelihood that the personality will remain tied to a particular place, and when that happens there is always the possibility that 'ghostly manifestations' will occur.

So what happens when someone 'sees' a ghost? Well, as we know, the personality is a vibration at a certain frequency of energy, and that energy can affect the energy of the air around it. As a simple analogy here, think of being on a long straight road on a very hot day. Look in the distance, and you may see a heat haze rising from the road surface, and causing the air above the road to shimmer. What is happening is that the heat is so intense that the radiation off the road is having an effect on the light waves that are bringing the scene to your eyes, and so your brain is interpreting that as a shimmer. (It is the same sort of thing as what happens on television, where there is electrical interference in the atmosphere, which interferes with the ability of the set to decode the TV waves correctly.)

So in the case of a ghost, the energy of the personality is affecting the light waves in that area, and those who are particularly sensitive are likely to pick up that interference as an actual physical shape. The definition of that shape will depend on the sensitivity of the individual.

Children are particularly prone to seeing ghosts, as when they are born they usually have a strong connection to the energy level from which they have just come – 'Heaven' – and so are very sensitive, until gradually they lose that sensitivity, either by just losing interest or – more normally – by having it ridiculed out of them by adults who do not understand what is happening. In the cases where children are encouraged to discuss what they see and feel by their parents, many of them retain that natural gift into adult life, and may well become practising mediums.

My wife and I have often been asked to go to a house where the occupants were having un-nerving ghostly apparitions, and on one occasion there were six children in the family, and all were reporting having contacts with an 'other-worldly' being. We went into the kitchen, and found the 'ghost' of a lovely old lady, a previous owner of the house, who had never had any children of her own, but who had always loved having the children of neighbours round her – and she was really enjoying herself among so many children, most of whom could either 'see' or 'hear' her – or in some cases both. Once we had explained the situation to the parents, they were no longer worried by the unusual activities of the children, who all loved 'Granny'.

What is the difference between 'right- and left-brain activity?'

Medical scientists tell us that different parts of the brain control different activities. The left-hand side is concerned with logic, reasoning and calculation, whereas the right-hand side is more to do with sensitivity, intuition, emotion and compassion. For some strange reason, each side of the brain controls the opposite side of the body. This gives rise to the idea that people who are left-handed have a greater tendency to be artistic and creative. I don't know if that is a proven fact or not, but it certainly seems to be the case in all the left-handed people whom I know.

Now because logic and reasoning are thought of as masculine qualities, the left brain is called the 'masculine' side, while the right brain is the 'feminine' side.

Let me emphasise that 'masculine' and 'feminine' in this context does not necessarily tie up with the biological gender of the individual person: there are many very logical and calculating women, just as there are many intuitional men. However, it seems to be a fact that the side of the brain associated with masculine or feminine traits tends to be more developed in people of that same gender.

This would explain why boys and girls, from an early age, tend to choose different toys. Some adults decry this 'gender stereotyping', and try to force children to use non-specific toys – those which can interest either sex – and the latest trend is towards even allowing children to choose what sex they would prefer to be, and what way they would like to dress. Whether this social experiment is able to overcome the natural development of the child's brain remains to be seen. It could well lead to the appearance of a generation of very confused adults.

The Scientific Background

As far as Spiritualism is concerned, the difference between right- and left-brain activity is very important, as all mediumship is concerned with sensitivity to vibrations – and sensitivity is governed by the right brain. So it is more likely that women, who are generally more sensitive than men, with the right-brain more developed, become interested in Spiritualism in the first place, and then go on to train to become mediums.

To give a personal experience of this, over the years in our centre we have called on the services of probably thirty to forty mediums, but only five of those have been men. It wasn't a case of 'sex discrimination', merely a case of availability.

However, if this is so you might ask why most of the top mediums in the country – certainly those in the public eye – appear to be men? Is it because of the supposed 'glass ceiling' which often stops women getting the top jobs in trade and industry, or is it something else entirely? A possible answer may be that men – traditionally – have always been the leaders, the hunter gatherers, the ones who went out and provided for the family, while the women stayed at home and looked after the children. So when a man has an exceptional ability in anything, even psychic talent, he is more likely to be willing to try to go out and capitalise on it than a women of equal – or greater – capability would. Obviously there are notable exceptions to this, but it is certainly an idea worth thinking about.

Meditation

What is meditation?

Meditation is a practice which is designed to help the individual to separate the active mind from all the various concerns which occupy it in everyday life, so that the emotional sensitivity may start to operate. All of us have both a mental and an emotional side to our nature, but in daily life the mental side tends to dominate. We are continually thinking of what we are doing, planning what to do next, remembering how to do things, etc., and so the emotional side gets pushed to one side. It is only when we see or are told of something particularly heart-wrenching, or we remember something particularly poignant in our past – possibly a tragedy, or the departure of a dearly-beloved person who is no longer on Earth – that we allow the emotional side to take over.

However, if we want to develop possible spiritual gifts, we have to blot out all the mundane every-day thoughts, and start to give our emotional side free rein. This is often very difficult, as over the years we have been either conditioned as a child, or learned the hard way as an adult, to keep our sensitivity under control, and here we are doing exactly the opposite.

So a period of training is necessary to be able to switch over from one mode of operation – mental – to another – emotional – and this can be done in a variety of ways.

In some oriental disciplines – yoga, for instance – the trainee is instructed to focus mentally on a particular part of the body, often the top of the nose, between the eyes, and concentrate on that until all other thoughts are wiped from the mind. However, that is a very difficult thing to do for more than a minute or so, so in Spiritualist meditations a more 'user-friendly' approach is usually made. A detailed example of the approach usually used in Spiritualist circles is given in the chapter on 'How mediums are trained'.

Metaphysics

Metaphysics

Let us start off with a simple analogy. Two men stood, back to back, on the Equator at some place on the Earth's surface. One faced East, and the other West. Then they started to travel round the Earth. The further they travelled, the greater the distance in a straight line between them, until when they were a quarter of the way round they were at the greatest distance apart.

Then, however, as they continued their journey, they started to get closer to each other, until eventually, at the opposite side of the Earth to where they had started; they met face to face at what I will call 'the meeting point'.

This is very similar to what is happening to Science and Religion. Originally science and religion were thought of as different sides of the same study, and early scientists backed their findings with philosophical – what we would now call 'religious' – beliefs. Then in the Middle Ages the basic scientific ideas of the Christian Church – and particularly the idea that the Earth was the centre of the universe, and everything rotated round it – started to clash with what scientists were proving as facts.

Nicolaus Copernicus (1473 – 1543) formulated the theory that the planets revolved round the sun, and his book on it was published just before his death. Giordano Bruno (1548 – 1600) enlarged the theory but fell foul of the Catholic hierarchy and was burnt at the stake in 1600. Galileo (1564 – 1642) supported his views, but was forced to recant – go back on his ideas – and in 1633 was sentenced to house imprisonment for life. However, in 1609, working on an improvement of an existing drawing of a primitive telescope, he had created a much more powerful one, which eventually proved that scientists were right, and led to the Church admitting that it was wrong. That gave rise to an era where it was generally agreed that anything concerning the physical universe was the province of Science, whereas philosophical ideas were matters for Religion.

Broadly speaking, that is still the situation: religious people pay little attention to scientific facts – there are still fundamentalist Christians who believe in the literal truth of Biblical stories about the Creation – whereas most scientists dismiss religious concepts as fantasy. (In fact, one of the most influential of modern scientists calls anything to do with Spiritualism 'woo-woo stuff'.)

However, with modern scientific discoveries – and particularly ideas on Quantum Physics – some of the lines between religion and science are becoming very blurred, so much so that scientists are very close to reaching 'the meeting point', where they will find – to their horror – that they have finally proved the existence of 'God', or whatever term is appropriate in their mind-set.

However, by the time that they reach there, theologians – religious specialists – will still be very far away: most of them, in different religions all over the world, are still arguing about the precise name of the Creative Force.

One day, some enlightened members of both the scientific and the religious communities will realise that there is much to be gained in collaborating together on projects of common interest, for instance, in healing. Over the last hundred years or more, spiritual healers have been working on patients, and sometimes achieving miraculous results, which the scientific community in general have tried to debunk – and failing this, have simply ignored. Perhaps some brave scientists could be persuaded to put their reputations on the line by doing a scientific study of the work of some reputed healer or other, to try to establish exactly what – if anything – is happening.

Many studies have been done over the years to try to provide answers to the powers of mediums, but all have been aimed at discrediting the medium concerned. However, as Quantum Physics has now proved, even the results of scientific experiments can be twisted by the power of the thoughts and expectations of the experimenters, so perhaps it would be possible to find scientists who would be prepared to collaborate on projects without a prior expectation of the likely result. One can only hope so.

It could be asked why any scientist or theologian would ever want to enter into some sort of collaboration? The simple answer is that some of the most basic beliefs of Science and Religion are the same. (I can almost feel the shock and horror of any scientist or theologian who reads that, so I hasten to explain why it is true.)

More than sixty years ago I was a Bible student, and one passage in the Bible – two of the opening verses of the Gospel of St John – always puzzled me.

'In the beginning was the Word, and the Word was with God, and the Word was God',   and   'By him were all things made, and without him was nothing made which was made'.

What was 'the Word', and what on earth does that passage mean?

It was fifty years later, when writing a channelled book, that I was given the answer: the Word was 'energy'. So substituting 'energy' for 'the Word', the passage now reads:

'In the beginning (there) was energy, and energy was with God, and energy was God. By it were all things made, and without it was nothing made which was made.'

Now that makes complete sense. What St. John was stating was a very basic scientific fact.

So if that interpretation of the passage is correct, then what theologians say about God and what scientists say about energy should bear some resemblance to each other. So let's see if they do:

Scientists say that energy has always existed, and will always exist. Theologians say that God is eternal.

Scientists say that energy is infinite. Theologians say that God is infinite.

Scientists say that everything was produced out of energy. Theologians say that God created everything.

Scientists say that you cannot create or destroy energy. Theologians say that you cannot add to, or take away from, God.

Scientists say that although you cannot create or destroy energy, it can be changed into many different forms. Theologians say that God manifests himself in many different ways.

Even by looking at those few examples, it is fairly obvious that there is at least a very strong possibility that when scientists are talking about energy, and when theologians are talking about God, they are both talking about the same thing – although both sides would vehemently dispute the fact.

That is the start of a study of Metaphysics. Is it enough to inspire some scientists and theologians to think of what might possibly happen in collaboration? I don't know. However, if you are either a scientist or a theologian, I leave the thought as a seed in your mind.

Index

Index

U
Unconditional Love 16
United Spiritualists 114

V
vibrations 122

W
Wheel of Re-birth 24

Z
Zadkiel 15, 35, 53

www.ingramcontent.com/pod-product-compliance
Lightning Source LLC
LaVergne TN
LVHW051413080426
835508LV00022B/3059